The Gospel of Mark
Made Easy

PATRICK J. FLANAGAN

D0907682

PAULIST PRESS
New York/Mahwah, N.J.

Nihil obstat
Veronica Lawson, R.S.M.
Censor deputatus

Imprimatur
+Ronald A. Mulkearns, D.D.
Bishop of Ballarat, Victoria, Australia
22 November 1996

Cover design by Cindy Dunne.

Library of Congress Cataloging-in-Publication Data

Flanagan, Patrick J.
    The Gospel of Mark made easy / Patrick J. Flanagan.
        p.   cm.
    Includes bibliographical references.
    ISBN 0-8091-3728-3 (alk. paper)
    1. Bible. N.T. Mark—Commentaries. I. Title.
BS2585.3.F53   1997
226.3 ' 077—dc21   97-18541
                                                       CIP

Published by Paulist Press
997 Macarthur Boulevard
Mahwah, New Jersey 07430

Printed and bound in the
United States of America

TO

CYRIL CONNOLLY, M.S.C.

CONTENTS

PREFACE

This book is dedicated to Cyril Connolly, M.S.C., whom I have never met. I was ordained a priest on July 24th, 1960. In my eight years of seminary formation prior to that, scripture played no mean part. It was a major subject for seven of the eight years. Nevertheless, though the landmark encyclical *Divino Afflante Spiritu* of Pope Pius XII had appeared in 1943, it had no influence on our scripture course. So I emerged from the seminary nourished well with scripture, yet not nearly as well as I might have been. I was a moderate fundamentalist.

For the next twenty years, in spite of various In-services and the like, I coasted along on the scripture formation of those seminary days. Ever cautious, when I was first informed by a Presbyterian minister that Adam and Eve might have been symbolic rather than actual people, I quickly banished the thought from my mind with the judgment, "That's what you'd expect from a Presbyterian minister." When, a few years later, a Catholic priest made a similar observation to me, I began cautiously to admit the possibility of this into the framework of my careful conservatism. And so I continued along my way.

In the year 1979, I was pastor of Maryborough in Central Victoria, Australia, a town of about ten thousand people. I had, by dint of hard work, managed to complete the home visitation of my parishioners by the end of September, leaving the remaining quarter free to pursue other activities. Among those activities was to begin wading through a nearly three-foot-high pile of magazines and journals. As they would arrive, being too busy to digest them on the spot, I would add them to the pile waiting to be read. I began to read, hurriedly, not taking in much of what I read. It was an act of obsessive compulsion rather than of nourishment. The aim was to get the pile down to zero, so that I could tick off another job completed.

Among the magazines I used to receive was a monthly called *Annals*, produced by the Missionaries of the Sacred Heart. It used to carry a center section of catechetical material intended for students in years eleven and twelve.

During 1978–1979, this supplement had scripture as its focus. I read these magazines, including the scripture supplements, with the same hurried, nondigestive pace as I had done with the rest of the pile, until, in the October 1978 issue, I came to the first of three articles on John by Cyril Connolly, a lecturer in scripture at St. Paul's National Seminary, in Sydney.

Until I began to read the first of those articles I had sometimes expressed the opinion that John was "eating mushrooms" when he wrote his Gospel (and, most particularly when he wrote those passages that form a series of week-day Gospel readings in what I still term "the horror stretch" toward the end of Lent). Cyril Connolly introduced me to the plan of the Fourth Gospel. From that moment, the Gospel of John began to come alive for me. I had found a pearl, and I wanted to share my find with others. The discovery of John led inevitably to many more discoveries. Those articles of Cyril's piloted me into a world that had been there for a long time, an already familiar world to many, but for me a new world.

My entering into that world has greatly enriched my mind, my prayer, my preaching, and my understanding of the Catholic faith. And so Cyril Connolly, M.S.C., is one of the many persons to whom I owe an unpayable debt.

I am primarily a pastor, not a scholar. I think that I discovered for myself that each part of Mark's Galilean ministry ended with failure. Most of this book, however, depends on knowledge gleaned from others, and sometimes further developed. Foremost among them are Francis Moloney and Donald Senior, but there are very many others from whose research I have benefited, among whom are William Barclay, Karen Barta, Raymond Brown, Christopher Burdon, Eugenio Corsini, Arthur Dewey, Joanna Dewey, Michael Fallon, Elisabeth

Schüssler Fiorenza, Wilfred Harrington, Werner Kelber, John J. Kilgallen, Jack Dean Kingsbury, Eugene LaVerdiere, Burton L. Mack, Ralph Martin, Frank J. Matera, John Meier, Jerome Murphy-O'Connor, George T. Montague, Ched Myers, Jerome Neyrey, Caroline Osiek, Barbara Reid, David Rhoades, Donald Michie, Eduard Schweizer, Augustine Stock, and Vincent Taylor. Occasionally, the contribution has been because of my negative reaction to their viewpoint. For the most part, however, they have added to my knowledge of Mark or have provided me with leads I was able to pursue further.

My special thanks to Mark Coleridge, who urged me to write this book; and to Bryan Coffey, Barbara Reid, Veronica Lawson, Frank Moloney, and Mark Coleridge again, each of whom criticized, suggested, and helped along the way. Equal thanks to Enid and Brian Brasier and Margaret and Paul Naughtin, who (at my request) freely criticized my Mark-like grammar and made some other valuable suggestions.

Finally, I cannot express at all adequately my gratitude to Lawrence Boadt, C.S.P., of Paulist Press for his great patience with me. Early in my dealings with him, I succumbed to quite deep depression, brought on by the conditions of my work. His kindness to a total stranger living half a world away from him helped me to keep going.

Patrick J. Flanagan
April 25, 1996
The Feast of St. Mark

CHAPTER 1

WHAT IS A GOSPEL?

THE GOSPELS ARE NOT DIARIES

The Gospels are not diaries, and there is no need to be afraid of that. Fundamentalists are not a peculiar class of people separate from the rest of the human race. Fundamentalism is an aspect of the human search for security. It derives from the fear that, if I question anything, everything then becomes questionable and the foundations of my world may collapse.

When it comes to the Gospels, the fundamentalist in me makes me want to believe that anything the Gospels say about Jesus is reported with complete accuracy. The fundamentalist would make the Gospels into diary extracts, written down by an eyewitness. It can be shown easily from the Gospels themselves that they are not that kind of writing. Discovering this for the first time can make the discoverer very afraid. I need therefore to state clearly that, while the Gospels do not have the accuracy that a firsthand eyewitness is presumed to provide, we are setting out to discover that they are something much better.[1]

A number of examples will be given now of Gospels differing from one another in details of an event. Sometimes the differences are quite significant.

The Great Commandment

Below is the text of the Great Commandment as found in Mark, and then Matthew and Luke.

Mark 12:28–34

One of the scribes came near and heard them disputing with one another, and seeing that he answered them well, he asked him, "Which commandment is the first of all?" 29Jesus answered, "The first is, 'Hear, O Israel: the Lord our God, the Lord is one; 30you shall love the Lord your God with all your heart, and with all your soul, and with all your mind, and with all your strength.' 31The second is this, 'You shall love your neighbor as yourself.' There is no other commandment greater than these." 32Then the scribe said to him, "You are right, Teacher; you have truly said that 'he is one, and besides him there is no other'; 33and 'to love him with all the heart, and with all the understanding, and with all the strength,' and 'to love one's neighbor as oneself,'—this is much more important than all whole burnt offerings and sacrifices." 34When Jesus saw that he answered wisely, he said to him, "You are not far from the kingdom of God." After that no one dared to ask him any question.

Matthew 22:34–40

When the Pharisees heard that he had silenced the Sadducees, they gathered together, 35and one of them, a lawyer, asked him a question to test him. 36"Teacher, which commandment in the law is the greatest?" 37He said to him, "'You shall love the Lord your God with all your heart, and with all your soul, and with all your mind.' 38This is the greatest and first commandment. 39And a second is like it: 'You shall love your neighbor as yourself.' 40On these two commandments hang all the law and the prophets."

Luke 10:25–28

Just then a lawyer stood up to test Jesus. "Teacher," he said, "what must I do to inherit eternal life?" 26He said to him, "What is written in the law? What do you read there?" 27He answered, "You shall love the Lord your God with all your heart, and with all your soul, and with all your strength, and with all your mind; and your neighbor as yourself." 28And he said to him, "You have given the right answer; do this, and you will live."

Notice, first, who asks Jesus the question. Each Gospel has a slightly different way of describing the questioner. In this instance, the differences are mainly a matter of emphasis. But notice now who answers the question by stating the Great Commandment. In Luke, the lawyer provides the answer to his own question. On the level of literal historical accuracy, Luke cannot be reconciled with Mark and Matthew. If we are going to say that each account is completely accurate, then we are forced to say that Luke is describing an episode different from the one in Matthew and Mark. It might be satisfactory to do that in the case of this one single episode; but if the fundamentalist in me is going to adopt this solution every time there is some conflict between different Gospels, then I am going to have to say that most events described in the Gospels occurred more than once. It makes much more sense for me to question my fundamentalism.

Notice also the placing of this event in the Gospels. In Mark and Matthew, the episode occurs in Jerusalem, amid controversy, in the last week of Jesus' life. In Luke it occurs somewhere on the journey from Galilee to Jerusalem. Notice finally that, whereas seemingly in Luke and certainly in Matthew the questioner is hostile toward Jesus, in Mark Jesus praises the scribe.

Two further examples will be given, comparing Mark and Matthew.

The Calming of the Storm

Mark 6:45–52	Matthew 14:22-33
Immediately he made his disciples get into the boat and go on ahead to the other side, to Bethsaida, while he dismissed the crowd. [46]After saying farewell to them, he went up on the mountain to pray.	Immediately he made the disciples get into the boat and go on ahead to the other side, while he dismissed the crowds. [23]And after he had dismissed the crowds, he went up the mountain by himself to pray. When evening came, he was there alone, [24]but by this time the boat, battered by the waves, was far from the land, for the wind was against them. [25]And early in the morning he came walking
[47]When evening came, the boat was out on the sea, and he was alone on the land. [48]When he saw that they were straining at the oars against an adverse wind, he came towards them	

early in the morning, walking on the sea. He intended to pass them by. [49]But when they saw him walking on the sea, they thought it was a ghost and cried out; [50]for they all saw him and were terrified. But immediately he spoke to them and said, "Take heart, it is I; do not be afraid." [51]Then he got into the boat with them and the wind ceased. And they were utterly astounded, [52]for they did not understand about the loaves, but their hearts were hardened.

[*Peter's walking on the water is not found in Mark.*]

toward them on the sea. [26]But when the disciples saw him walking on the sea, they were terrified, saying, "It is a ghost!" And they cried out in fear. [27]But immediately Jesus spoke to them and said, "Take heart, it is I; do not be afraid."

[28]Peter answered him, "Lord, if it is you, command me to come to you on the water." [29]He said, "Come ." So Peter got out of the boat, started walking on the water, and came toward Jesus. [30]But when he noticed the strong wind, he became frightened, and beginning to sink, he cried out, "Lord, save me!" [31]Jesus immediately reached out his hand and caught him, saying to him, "You of little faith, why did you doubt?" [32]When they got into the boat, the wind ceased. [33]And those in the boat worshipped him, saying, "Truly you are the Son of God."

In this episode, Matthew has an important note about Peter that is found nowhere in Mark. Of even greater significance, the reaction of the disciples to Jesus' walking on the water is very different in the two Gospels. In Mark the disciples, their hearts hardened, are simply baffled. In Matthew they say "Truly, You are the Son of God."

In the second example below notice that the *tendency* in Matthew, as against the tendency in Mark, is similar to that in the episode above.

The Yeast of the Pharisees

Mark 8:14–21	Matthew 16:5-12
Now the disciples had forgotten to bring any bread; and they had only one loaf with them in the boat. [15]And	When the disciples reached the other side, they had forgotten to bring any bread. [6]Jesus said to them, "Watch

he cautioned them, saying, "Watch out—beware of the yeast of the Pharisees and the yeast of Herod." [16]They said to one another, "It is because we have no bread." [17]And becoming aware of it, Jesus said to them, "Why are you talking about having no bread? Do you still not perceive or understand? Are your hearts hardened? [18]Do you have eyes, and fail to see? Do you have ears, and fail to hear? And do you not remember? [19]When I broke the five loaves for the five thousand, how many baskets full of broken pieces did you collect?" They said to him, "Twelve." [20]"And the seven for the four thousand, how many baskets full of broken pieces did you collect?" And they said to him, "Seven." [21]Then he said to them, "Do you not yet understand?"

out, and beware of the yeast of the Pharisees and Sadducees." [7]They said to one another, "It is because we have brought no bread." [8]And becoming aware of it, Jesus said, "You of little faith, why are you talking about having no bread? [9]Do you still not perceive? Do you not remember the five loaves for the five thousand, and how many baskets you gathered? [10]Or the seven loaves for the four thousand, and how many baskets you gathered? [11]How could you fail to perceive that I was not speaking about bread? Beware of the yeast of the Pharisees and Sadducees!" [12]Then they understood that he had not told them to beware of the yeast of bread, but of the teaching of the Pharisees and Sadducees.

There is a minor discrepancy between these two accounts. In Mark Jesus speaks of the yeast of the Pharisees and of *Herod;* in Matthew he speaks of the yeast of the Pharisees and of the *Sadducees.* But there is also a major discrepancy. In Mark the disciples do not understand; in Matthew they do.

Another comparison is given below. It is from the beginning of Jesus' ministry.

Jesus Calls Disciples

Mark 1:14–20

Now after John was arrested, Jesus came to Galilee, proclaiming the good news of God, [15]and saying, "The time is fulfilled, and the kingdom of God has come near; repent, and believe in the good news."

[16]As Jesus passed along the Sea of Galilee, he saw Simon and his brother

John 1:35–42

The next day John again was standing with two of his disciples, [36]and as he watched Jesus walk by, he exclaimed, "Look, here is the Lamb of God!" [37]The two disciples heard him say this, and they followed Jesus. [38]When Jesus turned and saw them following, he said to them, "What are

Andrew casting a net into the sea—for they were fishermen. [17]And Jesus said to them, "Follow me and I will make you fish for people." [18]And immediately they left their nets and followed him. [19]As he went a little farther, he saw James son of Zebedee and his brother John, who were in their boat mending the nets. [20]Immediately he called them; and they left their father Zebedee in the boat with the hired men, and followed him.

you looking for?" They said to him, "Rabbi" (which translated means Teacher), "where are you staying?" [39]He said to them, "Come and see." They came and saw where he was staying, and they remained with him that day. It was about four o'clock in the afternoon. [40]One of the two who heard John speak and followed him was Andrew, Simon Peter's brother. [41]He first found his brother Simon and said to him, "We have found the Messiah" (which is translated Anointed). [42]He brought Simon to Jesus, who looked at him and said, "You are Simon son of John. You are to be called Cephas" (which is translated Peter).

The setting in Mark is by the Sea of Galilee; the setting in John is near the River Jordan. And the accounts bear hardly any resemblance to each other. Actually, these two episodes are read at Mass on consecutive Sundays of Year B. John is the Gospel on the second Sunday, and Mark on the third Sunday.

Take out your New Testament now and compare Mk 11:15–17 with Jn 2:13–22. They are clearly about the same event, usually referred to as Jesus' cleansing the Temple. But their tone is very different. Mark's account could be labeled "Jesus closes the Temple." Equally John's account could be called "Jesus, the Temple of God." Each gives a different *meaning* to the event. A mere comparison of the position of each episode in its Gospel brings out a startling difference. In Mark, it is in the final, fateful week of Jesus' life. In John it is near the beginning of Jesus' ministry. Yet in both it takes place during Jesus' first visit to Jerusalem.

Finally, read the last chapter of Luke and the first chapter of Acts. There is a quite striking difference. In Luke 24 all the events seem to occur on Easter Sunday. In Acts 1, Jesus' appearances to his disciples are spread over forty days. Luke wrote both the Gospel and Acts. The one author, addressing different theological-pastoral needs, feels free to handle the same material quite differently.

Nearly all scripture scholars think (and their arguments are quite convincing) that when Matthew and Luke wrote their Gospels, each had before him Mark's Gospel and made extensive use of it.[2] If Matthew had Mark's account before him as he wrote and deliberately altered it, it can safely be concluded that literal accuracy was not Matthew's primary concern. If we can conclude that about Matthew, then perhaps we can draw the same conclusion about each of the Gospel writers, including Mark, the first of them. Indeed, there are incidents in Mark's narrative that, if taken wholly literally, have an unlikely quality about them. But if these incidents are read in the light of Mark's overall intention, their unlikeliness becomes quite insignificant.

While the Gospels do give us facts about Jesus, literal accuracy was not their primary concern. The Gospels are not diaries, and, although they are about the life of Jesus, they are not biographies either. We do not know from any of the Gospels the exact year or day of Jesus' birth; nor the exact day or year of his death (though we do know that it was on a Friday at Passover); nor do we know exactly how old Jesus was when he died.

If the Gospels are not primarily diaries or biographies or collections of facts about Jesus, then what are they?

FAILURE . . .

Some readers may not know that the present ending of Mark's Gospel (Mk 16:9–20) was not written by Mark. Mark's Gospel ends rather disappointingly at 16:8. It *seems* to be unfinished. Consequently, there were various attempts—at least three survive—to supply a fitting ending for Mark. One of these endings has been accepted as part of the New Testament. It is canonical, part of God's word, but Mark did not write it. A simple discerning reading of it is enough to show that vv. 9–20 cannot be a continuation of vv. 1–8. In fact they distract from Mark's purpose.

Here is the ending of Mark's Gospel as Mark intended it to be:

Mark 16:1–8. When the Sabbath was over, Mary Magdalene, and Mary the mother of James, and Salome bought spices, so that they might go and anoint him. [2]And very early on the first day of the week, when the sun had risen, they went to the tomb. [3]They had been saying to one another, "Who will roll away the stone for us from the entrance to the tomb?" [4]When they looked up, they saw that the stone, which was very large, had already been rolled back. [5]As they entered the tomb, they saw a young man, dressed in a white robe, sitting on the right side; and they were alarmed. [6]But he said to them, "Do not be alarmed; you are looking for Jesus of Nazareth, who was crucified. He has been raised; he is not here. Look, there is the place they laid him. [7]But go, tell his disciples and Peter that he is going ahead of you to Galilee; there you will see him, just as he told you." [8]So they went out and fled from the tomb, for terror and amazement had seized them; and they said nothing to anyone, for they were afraid.

Notice that the women have been given the task of announcing Jesus risen. But they fail to do this, because they are afraid. Mark quite deliberately ends his Gospel with *failure*. It seems a strange way to end the book that he has titled "The beginning of the Good News about Jesus, the Christ, the Son of God."[3] Strange Good News!

A careful reading of Mark reveals that his Gospel does not only *end* with failure; it is also punctuated by failure along the way. In the first half of the Gospel—Jesus' ministry in Galilee—each section ends with failure:

Galilee I (1:14–3:6)

Jesus' ministry appears to begin well. He sets out to establish the reign of God. There is great enthusiasm for him, but opponents quickly emerge, until at 3:6 we read: "The Pharisees went out and immediately conspired with the Herodians against him, how to destroy him."

Galilee II (3:7–6:6)

This second part of Jesus' ministry in Galilee has several phases. It leads to a lengthy segment in which Jesus' power is revealed: power over demons, over the forces of nature, over sickness, and over death itself. But, at the end of the section, faced with the refusal of human hearts, Jesus becomes powerless: "And he could do no deed of power there, except that he laid his hands on a few sick people and cured them. And he was amazed at their unbelief" (6:5–6).

Galilee III (6:7–8:21)

As this section develops, it becomes apparent that not only is Jesus unable to get the Pharisees or the crowds to see; even his chosen disciples are blind: "And becoming aware of it, Jesus said to them, 'Why are you talking about having no bread? Do you still not perceive or understand? Are your hearts hardened? Do you have eyes, and fail to see? Do you have ears, and fail to hear? And do you not remember? When I broke the five loaves for the five thousand, how many baskets full of broken pieces did you collect?' They said to him, 'Twelve.' 'And the seven for the four thousand, how many baskets full of broken pieces did you collect?' And they said to him, 'Seven.' Then he said to them, 'Do you not yet understand?'" (8:17–21)

Once we pass the halfway mark, the story becomes shot through with failure. Jesus has been unable by his ministry to establish the reign of God. The leadership plots against him. The crowds do not understand. The apostles are a strange mixture of loyalty to Jesus and opposition to his vision. The failure of the disciples is the most marked of all. In the person of Jesus, God walks among his people. The power of God is seen in him, and yet no one realizes who he is.

In the title that Mark gave to his story (a title that eventually was incorporated into the body of the Gospel as Mk 1:1), he designates Jesus by two titles: "the Christ" and "the Son of God." A question runs through the story line of the Gospel: "Who is this man?" Not until the halfway mark of the Gospel does anyone call Jesus "the Christ." That person is Peter. At last someone would seem to recognize who is among them. But even Peter sees poorly. Immediately after Peter recognizes, Jesus begins to teach what it means to be the Christ. But Peter tries to teach Jesus; the pupil sets out to teach the teacher, so that Jesus calls Peter "you Satan."

The title "the Christ" is the lesser of the two titles by which Mark designates Jesus. In Mark's story not one human being penetrates to the reality of Jesus' divine identity as the Son of God until the end. Despite all Jesus' works of power, no one sees—until he hangs dead on the cross. And then the one who realizes is a complete outsider to the story, a pagan, the Roman centurion. He has not seen any of Jesus' works of power. He has not heard him teach. How, then, does he recognize who Jesus is? Mark says, simply and enigmatically, "The centurion, who was standing in front of him, seeing *how* he had died, said 'Truly, this man was the Son of God.'"

Mark has told a story that is replete with mess and failure, a story that ends with failure, a story that asks us to look not at Jesus the man of power, not at Jesus the teacher, not even at Jesus risen, but at Jesus hanging defeated and abandoned on a cross. And he calls it all "the beginning of the Good News"! What caused Mark to present the story of Jesus in this way?

ROME, SHORTLY BEFORE 70 C.E.

Christianity may have reached Rome as early as 40 C.E., only a decade after Jesus died and rose from the dead. Who first preached Jesus there we simply do not know, just as we do not know who first brought the gospel to Antioch or Alexandria or to the other great centers of the Roman Empire. We can safely presume that the first evangelist of Rome was a Jew newly returned from Judea, where he or she had been converted to Christianity. The pagan historian Suetonius, in his life of the emperor Claudius, mentions that in 49 C.E., because of disturbances among

them instigated by a certain "Chrestus," Jews were expelled from
Rome. (Two of these Jews were Priscilla and Aquila. Their expulsion is mentioned in Acts 18:2.) It is not farfetched to read this as
a reference to strife of some kind caused by the spread of the
gospel in Rome.

There was a strong Jewish community in Rome, of long standing. Jews are mentioned as living in Rome as early as 139 B.C.E.[4]
In 63 B.C.E. the Roman general Pompey entered Jerusalem with his
army and went right into the Holy of Holies of the Temple, thus
declaring Rome's mastery over Judea. To ensure that the Jews
would respect their new overlords, Pompey took hostages back to
Rome to be settled there. He also brought many Jews home to be
sold into slavery. Presumably the hostages came from leading
families in Judea, and they soon became leading families among
the Jews of Rome also. Whether for that or for some other reason,
the links between Jewry in Rome and in Judea were very strong.
Although they were living far away in Rome, Jerusalem with its
Temple was their real home. The Jews in Rome who became
Christians would naturally have retained this Temple centered-
ness in their spirituality.

As happened elsewhere, some of Rome's pagan population
were also converted to Christ. And, as happened in other places,
their becoming part of the church together with Jews brought
tensions. While some would perhaps willingly submit to the
Jewish law, others would have balked; at the very least they would
have been uneasy about submitting to circumcision. The civilized
world generally thought circumcision to be an abomination.
Some of the Jewish Christians would have looked down their
noses at the pagan Johnny-come-lately Christians, who lacked the
heritage of Judaism. Conversely, some of the Gentile Christians
despised the Jewish Christians for clinging to outmoded obser-
vances. Possibly, after the expulsion of the Jews by Claudius, the
church in Rome was for a few years exclusively Gentile. When,
after the emperor's anger abated, the Jewish-Christians returned,
they may have found a Gentile community none too happy about
Jewish-Christians reasserting their dominance.

For sensitive Jewish consciences there were some very real
problems. The church in Rome, as elsewhere, used to meet in

houses. In the course of a shared meal, the Eucharist was celebrated. The kind of food provided by Gentile Christians could
create deep concern for Jewish Christians strict about their heritage. It might not be *kosher*.

The Christians of Rome felt strong enough to indulge in dis-
sent; they enjoyed the luxury of squabbles. And both Jewish and
Gentile Christians, basking in the light of Easter, of having found
assurance of God's salvation, could feel superior to the rest of
Rome's populace. Unlike these outsiders, the Christians enjoyed a
secure vision about God and about human destiny. They felt
strong. Among the churches, the church in Rome counted enough
for Paul to have felt the need to write (in 57 C.E.) his letter to the
Romans. That letter was needed to clarify his own understanding
of the relationship of Gentiles to the law of Moses. He had dealt
with the matter rather hot-headedly in his letter to the Galatians.

About 61 C.E. Paul came to Rome, and about the same time
Peter also came to Rome. The church in Rome could feel itself to
be both important and influential. Under the rule of the emperor
Nero, Rome was prospering, and the Christians of Rome, whether
Jew or Gentile, had reason to be happy about life.

Then, in 64 an event occurred that was to change all that. A fire
broke out in Rome's slum area and got out of control. It burned
for six days. Ten out of Rome's fourteen districts—about three-
quarters of the city—were destroyed before the fire was put out. It
was common knowledge that Nero had been hoping to pull down
the slum areas and rebuild. It was not long before tongues began
to wag, and Nero was in trouble. He needed to find a scapegoat.
The Jews, detested by the populace at large because they insisted
on being different, would have provided a very convenient scapegoat. The Jewish quarter had not been touched by the fire.
Fortunately for them, they had a defender at the imperial court.
Nero's wife, Poppaea, looked on the Jews favorably.

Nero found his scapegoat in "the new superstition," the
Christians. At this point it would be best to quote from the pagan
historian Tacitus:

> But all human efforts, all the lavish gifts of the emperor, and the
> propitiations of the gods, did not banish the sinister belief that the

conflagration was the result of an order. Consequently, to get rid of the report, Nero fastened the guilt, and inflicted the most exquisite tortures, on a class hated for their abominations, called Christians by the populace. Christus, from whom the name had its origin, suffered the extreme penalty during the reign of Tiberius at the hands of one of our procurators, Pontius Pilate, and a deadly superstition, thus checked for the moment, again broke out, not only in Judea, the first source of the evil, but also in the City, where all things hideous and shameful from every part of the world meet and become popular.

Accordingly, an arrest was first made of all who confessed; then, upon their information, an immense multitude was convicted, not so much of the crime of arson, as of hatred of the human race. Mockery of every sort was added to their deaths. Covered with the skins of wild beasts, they were torn by dogs and perished, or were nailed to crosses, or were doomed to the flames. These served to illuminate the night when the daylight failed. Nero had thrown open his gardens for the spectacle, and was exhibiting a show in the circus, while he mingled with the crowd in the dress of a charioteer or drove about in a chariot. Hence, even for criminals who deserved extreme and exemplary punishment, there arose a feeling of compassion; for it was not, as it seemed, for the public good, but to glut one man's cruelty, that they were being destroyed.[5]

"Upon their information" does not mean that the Christians arrested first immediately volunteered the names of other Christians. Almost certainly they were questioned under torture. Nevertheless, it does mean that some had betrayed their fellow Christians. It is likely that the best known of the Christians would have belonged to long-established Jewish families. If, when the torture became severe enough, they were ready to reveal the names of other Christians, they would naturally reveal the names of Christians who belonged to a different faction. The picture can be filled out further. Some Christians fled Rome. Others, when put to the test, abandoned the faith. You had Christians no longer wanting to associate with other Christians, especially those likely to be known to the authorities. You had "brother betraying brother to death" (Mk 13:12). The luxury of factionalism and family in-fighting had become a destructive power. From a phrase used by Clement, writing from Rome to Corinth in the year 96

C.E., it appears that Peter and Paul were betrayed by fellow Christians. Victims of the church's in-fighting, they were betrayed out of "jealous envy." Both leaders were martyred in Rome in the year 65. To a church that had basked in the light of Easter, Calvary had become no longer something that happened three decades previously. It was present now. Christians in Rome were being crucified, or put to death in other ways equally barbaric.

In short, this community that prided itself on its strength and importance found that, faced with the cross, it was weak. It had failed. It was a bruised and battered mess, licking its wounds, feeling sorry for itself.

Yet still the factions continued and new questions arose. The persecution over, some of the defectors wished to return. Some who had not defected did not want them back. Others said that the church had no power to reconcile them.

For the Jewish Christians a further cause for fear had arisen. In 66, Judea revolted against the rule of Rome. Crushing the revolt had not proved easy for Rome. Consequently, when Jerusalem did finally capitulate, a punishment that was both vengeful and exemplary would be exacted. To Jewish Christians, just as much as to other Jews in Rome, the thought of Jerusalem and its Temple being destroyed was cause for more than dismay: it looked like the end of everything.

There were other events that made it appear to all that their world was ending. In 68, his despotism having turned everybody against the once-popular young emperor, and the Roman senate having condemned him to death *in absentia*, Nero committed suicide. There followed a period of total anarchy. For about a hundred years prior to 31 B.C.E., even while growing as a world power, Rome was being torn by civil war. The triumph of Caesar Augustus in 31 B.C.E. had at last put an end to this hemorrhaging strife. The *Pax Augusta*—the peace that Augustus had brought to the empire—was celebrated everywhere. But now, with the death of Nero, peace had abandoned the city. The Praetorian Guard installed Galba as emperor. Then, dissatisfied with him, they murdered him and named Otho, governor of a province in Spain, as emperor. The army in Germany decided that it had as much right as the Praetorian Guard to appoint emperors of Rome. It chose Vitellius, who marched into Italy. As Vitellius advanced, Otho committed suicide. The armies on the Danube decided that Vitellius was not suitable, so they chose Vespasian, who was then conducting the siege of Jerusalem. Vespasian marched on Rome, defeated and killed Vitellius, and asked the senate, the legitimate authority, to appoint him as emperor. This they did. When Vespasian lifted the siege of Jerusalem to return to Rome, the Jews found a short-lived respite. But soon Vespasian's son, Titus, recommenced the siege that would end with massive destruction in Jerusalem, and with the Temple put to the torch. The year had seen four emperors. Vespasian was in fact to inaugurate a new peace; but to those living in Rome early in 69 C.E. that was not apparent.

The person we know as Mark set out to address Rome's confused Christian community in its need, not by preaching sermons or writing rousing hymns, nor by holding seminars, forming subcommittees and task forces, but by telling again a story, the story of Jesus. The story is told in such a way as to force the Christians to notice things they already knew but preferred not to see.[6] In the joy of Easter, they had forgotten the cross, so that, when the crucified one had called them to take up the cross, they had failed. Mark has, though, no desire to sit in judgment. Mark holds out to this community that has failed the story of the failure of all when God walked among us.

While Mark emphasizes the failures at the beginning of the gospel's entry into history, his purpose is not to condemn, but to engender hope. Mark's Gospel is a call to accept the cross. Until we have seen the cross, and that means accepting it in our lives, we can know neither Jesus nor his Father. In writing thus, Mark was the author of a new kind of literature. A Gospel is the story of Jesus told not as a tribute, nor as biography, nor to preserve memories of Jesus, but to speak to people in their need.

ABOUT THE AUTHOR

The early church writers who mention the authorship of the first Gospel attribute it to Mark. Later, it was generally presumed that this Mark is the John Mark whose mother had a house in Jerusalem and who was sometimes a companion of Paul and of Barnabas (see Acts 12:12; 13:5, 13; 15:38). While there is no absolutely convincing reason to deny this, the author did not sign his (or her) name to the book. As far as its own author is concerned, the Gospel is anonymous. The same is true of the other Gospels. Yet from the story itself, we can make some surmises about the author: (1) Behind the style of writing is a strongly Aramaic background. Aramaic was the main language of Palestine in the time of Jesus. The author was probably a native of Palestine. The author's mental home is the earthy and colorful world of the Semites. (2) Though the Gospel was written in Greek, Greek being the *lingua franca* of the Roman Empire, it is a rather rough Greek. Greek was very much a second language to the author, a language with which he was not very comfortable. There are plenty of occasions where, as they copied from Mark, either Matthew or Luke or both found it necessary to correct his grammar. Hippolytus, a second-century Roman writer, described Mark as stump-fingered, almost certainly referring to Mark's Greek, not to some physical defect. (3) Rather too frequently Mark used Latinisms; that is, he used words that were not really Greek words at all, but Latin words transliterated into, written to look like, Greek words. Latin was spoken very little outside Italy, which suggests that Mark had lived in a Christian community in Italy long enough to have acquired some familiarity with Latin.

If the author did not sign his name, neither did he state the date or place of writing. The early tradition names Rome as the place where this Gospel was written. While it cannot be proved absolutely, Rome *after* the persecution of Nero but *before* the fall of Jerusalem fits the Gospel. The Gospel of Mark is at home there.

Excursus 1
Rome as the Home of the Gospel
and Mark as the Author

Sometimes Mark uses Aramaic words. Except for *Amen, Hosanna, Gehenna,* and Gethsemane and rabbi, he always supplies immediately a translation. The words he does not translate were evidently known to his readers. His having to translate most Aramaic words is a strong argument against those who would maintain that Mark was written not in Rome but in Galilee; for, apart from Rome, Galilee is the only other place ever proposed seriously as the place where this Gospel was written (although some scholars, recognizing that it is not plausible for a work written in Galilee to have mistakes about the geography of Galilee, have suggested that Mark was written somewhere in Syria farther north than Galilee itself.

As has been noted above, Mark did not sign his name to the Gospel; neither did he date it nor state the place of writing. It is impossible then to prove absolutely that Mark wrote the Gospel in Rome early in 69 C.E.

Those who argue for Galilee adduce mainly the importance of Galilee in Mark's Gospel. Most of Jesus' ministry is placed there. Jesus never enters Jerusalem until the last week of his life. But this format of ministry in Galilee—journey to Jerusalem—ministry in Jerusalem serves Mark's terse dramatic style. By the time Mark wrote his Gospel, the art of writing plays to be read, not acted, had been established. The playwright Seneca wrote dramas of this kind. The Gospel of Mark has all the earmarks of such a writing. Dramatic composition is more than sufficient to justify Mark's stylized story line.

Besides, Matthew and Luke would have known that Jesus' ministry fluctuated between Galilee and Judea (as it does in John). Yet they found Mark's basic structure ministry in Galilee, journey to Jerusalem, Jerusalem—useful enough to have copied it. The importance of Galilee for Mark is not geographical. Galilee is symbolic of the ambiguity of real life, over against the comfortable orthodoxy of Jerusalem. Galilee is where the kingdom must be preached and lived.

A small section of chapter 13, the apocalyptic discourse, is more easily understood if Galilee is the place of composition. It is, however, dangerous to argue from a couple of verses alone; and particularly when they are in the middle of a notoriously difficult mode of writing. If I may take a parallel case, a skilled debater might *prove* from Mt 21:7 (where the author has Jesus riding on both a donkey *and* its colt) that Matthew does not recognize Semitic parallelism; and therefore he was not only not a Jew, but not Semitic at all. However, against this lone solitary text, there is much in Matthew's Gospel to suggest that its author was Semitic. Nearly all scholars, while recognizing that 21:7 creates a difficulty, place that text on hold, and presume that Matthew was a Semite.

The arguments for Rome, besides the early attestation of all authorities, can be summarized as follows:

1. The Gospel demands a situation of persecution. The only *known* persecution before that under Domitian in the nineties is the persecution in Rome under Nero in the sixties. The sporadic episodes mentioned by Luke in Acts do not qualify.

2. The situation of a community that failed in the persecution makes sense of Mark's emphasis on failure. We know from the later persecutions that some Christians failed then. The evidence provided by those experiences as well as the testimony provided by Tacitus and *1 Clement* is sufficient to let us presume that, in Nero's—the first real persecution of Christians—there was failure as well as heroism; and that the community left in shock.

3. Mark's general tendency to translate Aramaic words argues strongly against Galilee. Aramaic was the first language of most Galileans and would have been the second language of those Galileans for whom Greek was the first language.

4. Mark's explaining some Jewish customs argues that some in his community do not know much about Judaism. This fits Rome far better than Galilee.

5. Mark (7:26) refers to a woman as a Syrophoenician. There were two Phoenicias. One was in northern Africa, centered on Carthage, not that far by sea from Italy. The other was in Syria (actually modern day Lebanon) just above Galilee. If Mark is writing in Rome, it makes perfect sense to specify Syrophoenicia. If he is writing in Galilee, it makes no sense at all.

6. In the episode of the widow's mite (12:42) Mark specifies the coin by mentioning "two lepta, which make a kodrans." The kodrans was used in Italy, and it was not in circulation in Asia Minor. On the other hand, the bronze lepton was the smallest Jewish coin. It was not in circulation in Italy; hence Mark's need to give a Roman equivalent.

7. Mark has numerous Latinisms. It is possible, without supposing Rome as the place of writing, to explain how Mark might have come by each one of these Latinisms. The sheer quantity of them is not so easily explained unless we suppose that Mark had Latin as one of his languages and wrote in a Latin-speaking area. See chapter 9, n. 29 about Mark 15:15. In at least that instance, Mark is more comfortable with Latin than with Greek.

8. In the divorce question (10:12) Mark mentions a woman divorcing her husband. It was simply not possible in Jewish Law for a woman to divorce her husband. The most an aggrieved woman could hope for was that the court would order her husband to divorce her. Jesus, therefore,

would not have dealt with the question of a woman divorcing her husband. Neither would Mark if he were writing in Galilee.

Many scholars no longer believe that John Mark was the author of the Gospel of Mark. Speaking for myself, my big question is, How could one John Mark, native of Jerusalem, have learned to write so dramatically? The most likely answer is that John Mark did not write this Gospel, but this may not be the correct answer. Perennially the argument reappears that a bard from Stratford-on-Avon could not possibly have written *Macbeth, Julius Caesar, Hamlet, King Lear,* and so on.

NOTES

1. In fact, diaries do not and cannot present mirror accuracy. In writing a diary entry, the mere act of deciding what to include and what to exclude involves interpreting what is and what is not important about the day.

2. Matthew, Luke, or both of them improve many times Mark's rough grammar. There is not a single instance of Mark correcting Matthew or Luke's grammar. It makes sense, if you are copying from someone, to correct their mistakes. It makes no sense at all to worsen someone's grammar. This is a very convincing reason, one of many, for saying that Mark wrote first, and Matthew and Luke made use of Mark in writing their Gospels.

3. The second title, Son of God, is missing from some ancient manuscripts of Mark. The branch of scripture studies that, by comparing various texts, sets out to establish the author's original text is called textual criticism. The term *criticism,* when used in scripture studies, does not mean "finding fault with" but making judgments or decisions (criticize comes from the Greek *krinō,* "I judge"). The standard Greek text of the New Testament is known as Nestle-Aland. It has long treated the second title as doubtful. But in its 26th edition, it finally accepted that "Son of God" was part of Mark's original text.

The title Son of God presents a second problem here and in 15:39. The title appears without the definite article. The English language has both the definite article and the indefinite article. Greek has a definite article but no indefinite article. Latin incidentally has neither. When the definite article is present, it is clearly meant. When, however, it is absent, the context and usage tell the reader whether definite or indefinite is intended. In this case the difference is quite large: *A* son of God might be a term of praise for an outstandingly good person. *The* Son of God is a unique title. Mark intends "the" both here and in chapter 15. His general usage through the Gospel is clear. Besides, to have "a son of God" following "Christ" is anticlimactic. See below, chapter 9, note 36.

4. See John Meier and Raymong Brown, *Antioch and Rome* (New York: Paulist, 1983), chapters 6–8

5. Quoted from *A New Eusebius: Documents Illustrating the History of the Church to AD 337*, ed. J. Stevenson, new ed. revised by W. H. C. Frend (London: SPCK, 1987), 2.

6. Mark presumes that the readers are Christians and that they know more of the story than he is narrating. Otherwise statements such as 1:8, "He will baptize you with the Holy Spirit," a statement that is not fulfilled in Mark's narrative would be unintelligible.

CHAPTER 2

GETTING STARTED

We are setting out to know Jesus as Mark presents him to us: the Son of God, but fully human, and vivid in his humanity. In listening to Mark's Jesus we will find him teaching us what it means to be his followers. We want to hear Mark's message. We need to let his word, the word of God, enter our hearts.

For many reasons our task is not easy. We are not the group of Christians in Rome whom Mark first addressed. We can only try to imagine ourselves in their situation. Our native tongue is not the rough first-century Greek that Mark wrote; so we have to hear Mark secondhand in a translation, knowing that translations can never fully capture the original. There are more weighty difficulties too. Most of us have heard or read Mark many times, but in bits and pieces. One of the features of the Gospels is that, for the most part, each incident in the Gospel has a completeness about it. (To describe this quality of completeness scholars use the technical word *pericope*. It has practically the same meaning as the English word *episode*.) That is the way we are used to hearing Mark, in isolated and self-contained incidents. Mark, however, wrote a complete book. He did not just string together a lot of separate, unconnected episodes. We need to hear Mark as a whole story. Mark meant his Gospel to be read, or rather (because most of his audience would have had no opportunity to read) to be heard as a whole. So we need to hear Mark in its *wholeness*.

At this point, unless you have at sometime previously done so, you should put this book down and read Mark's Gospel, preferably in one sitting, as you might read any short book that is new to you. Remember to finish where Mark finished—at 16:8.

To help yourself follow Mark's plot, keep in mind that Mark structured his book in two halves of roughly equal length. They are joined by a short central section, usually called the linchpin. This both ends the first half and begins the second half. The first half ends at 8:21. The linchpin runs from 8:22 to 8:33, and the second half continues to the end of the Gospel. Running through the first half is an ever-present background question, "Who is this man?" Notice the different answers people give to this question. In the linchpin Peter supplies half of the answer that was given to us in the Gospel's title. He says, "You are the Christ." The question of Jesus' identity recedes into the background during the second half of the Gospel, not to be answered fully until Jesus' passion. The questions that dominate the second half of the Gospel are introduced in the linchpin: What does it mean to be the Christ? What does it mean to follow the Christ? This division of Mark is not something imposed on his story by scholars. Mark fully intended it. Augustine Stock has drawn up an impressive list of differences between the two halves.[1] Look for these themes as you read. In addition, make note of any things about the story that surprise you. You will be attempting to hear Mark for the first time. You will need patience. In a sense, hearing Mark without presuppositions would be far easier for a person who had never previously encountered the Gospels than it is for us. As we read Mark, we *think* that we already know him. So we will be inclined not to give to him full attention. Moreover, because of our familiarity with each of the Gospels, we are sometimes going to read into Mark things that are not in Mark, but in one of the other Gospels. Sometimes we will both see what is *not* there and not see what *is* there.

You have persevered to the end of Mark's story. Possibly you found it easy; more likely you found it heavy going. The story is very tight, swiftly moving, and packed. It is like a giant telegram. The Gospel of Mark is in fact a play, a drama, written not to be performed by several actors but to be proclaimed dramatically. In the late 1970s, a British actor, Alex McCowen, learned Mark by heart. For over two years, each night, on the London stage, to full houses, he simply proclaimed Mark's Gospel. He described Mark as "the greatest script I ever came upon." You have not been able to hear Mark that way. Even if you had there is still much of importance that you would miss, because you cannot fully live in the thought-world out of which Mark wrote. There are, for example, many scriptural allusions that Mark expected his audience to recognize; we need to have them pointed out to us.

As we embark now on a detailed study of Mark, you need to be aware of the danger of becoming sidetracked. From a commentary such as this, you may acquire many pieces of information about Mark, and yet at the end of it you may not have begun to grasp Mark's message. In my own case, as a beginner I studied two commentaries on Mark and learned many facts about his Gospel, about the times of Jesus and so on; but Mark did not come alive for me until I happened to attend a crash course given by Francis J. Moloney, in which we went right through Mark in one day. That day I caught for the first time the flow of Mark's Gospel, the development of its plot. Your primary aim must be to get the whole story and not become lost, unable to see the wood for the trees. As we move through the Gospel, keep revising and catching the movement of the story.

You may find it useful to set up your own "Mark book." Photocopy the Gospel (observing copyright laws) so that you can use a highlighter without damaging your Bible. Make your copy large enough for you to be able to write notes between the lines; but leave plenty of margin space for other notes.

We will begin now by studying the title and prologue.

THE TITLE AND PROLOGUE OF THE GOSPEL
(1:1–13)

The Title (1:1)

The beginning of the good news of Jesus *the* Christ, the Son of God.

The stark title with which Mark commences his story evokes the equally terse opening words of the book of Genesis, "In the *beginning* God created the heavens and the earth."

The Christ

In reading Mark's Gospel, you may have noticed that, although Mark designates Jesus by the title The Christ, Jesus himself appears to shun it. Jesus' reticence about being called Messiah is often termed the *messianic secret.* There was in Jesus' time a great variety of expectations about the coming Messiah. Jesus could not identify himself with many of these expectations, particularly with distorted expectations concerning the restoration of political power. Hence his reticence. When the messianic secret in Mark is examined carefully, however, it becomes apparent that Jesus' reticence is not only, nor even mainly, about the title Messiah. It has more to do with Jesus' identity, who he is. Moreover, Jesus sometimes commands silence when silence is not possible. Mark's use of the messianic secret is in part a literary device. Briefly, it means this: until we know Jesus crucified we do not know what "Christ" means; and the same is true about knowing his identity as the Son of God.

The Son of God

Some New Testament writings are described as having a *high* Christology, others a *low* Christology. If Jesus' being divine is strongly and clearly asserted, there is a high Christology. Most prominent among the high-Christology documents is the Gospel of John. If Jesus' being human is asserted strongly and his being divine is not apparent, we have a low Christology. In Mark, Jesus is very clearly human, but Mark's Christology is a high Christology. In fact, Raymond Brown states quite simply that all of the Gospels and all New Testament documents that touch on the subject present Jesus as divine.[2] For me, of the four Gospels, Mark strikes the best balance in its presentation of Jesus: he is clearly human, and yet clearly divine. Vincent Taylor has stated that

"Mark's Christology is a high Christology, as high as any in the New Testament, not excluding that of John. Behind a fully human life Deity is concealed; but it is visible for those who have eyes to see it in his personality, teaching and deeds."[3] For Mark the title Son of God is not another way of saying Messiah. Mark fully intends this title to be unique. Nowhere in the Old Testament is any individual ever called "the Son of God." It does not mean God's viceroy on earth. An identity with God is being stated, though stated for the most part obliquely, because the central theology of Mark, I repeat, is that the full meaning of Jesus and of his being the Son of God can be known only on Calvary. Nevertheless, readers should not take this to denote that Mark, or any New Testament book, contains a fully elaborated understanding of what is meant by calling Jesus divine.

I have inserted "the" into the title *the Christ*. The title usually reads simply "Jesus Christ," and there are several instances in the New Testament of the title Christ becoming part of Jesus' name. My insertion is to make the parallel between the two titles more obvious.

The Prologue (1:2-11)

[2]As it is written in **the prophet Isaiah**, "See, I am sending my messenger ahead of you, who will prepare your way; [3]the voice of one crying out in the wilderness: 'Prepare the way of the Lord, make his paths straight,'" [4]John the baptizer appeared in the wilderness, proclaiming a baptism of repentance for the forgiveness of sins. [5]And people from the whole Judean countryside and all the people of Jerusalem were going out to him, and were baptized by him in the river Jordan, confessing their sins. [6]Now John was clothed with camel's hair, with a leather belt around his waist, and he ate locusts and wild honey. [7]He proclaimed, "The **one who is more powerful than I** is coming after me; I am not worthy to stoop down and untie the thong of his sandals. [8]I have baptized you with water; but he will baptize you with the Holy Spirit." [9]In those days Jesus came from Nazareth of Galilee and was baptized by John in

the Jordan. [10]And just as he was coming up out of the water, he saw the heavens torn apart and the Spirit descending **like a dove** on him. [11]And a voice came from heaven, **"You are my Son, the Beloved; with you I am well pleased."** [12]And the Spirit immediately drove him out into the wilderness. [13]He was in the wilderness forty days, tempted by Satan; and he was with the wild beasts; and the angels waited on him.

In the space of twelve verses, the stage for Jesus' ministry is set. In these few telegrammatic lines Mark presents the ministry of John the Baptist, the baptism of Jesus, and his time of testing in the desert. Mark is creating the sense of God's breaking into the world. The prophet Isaiah had cried out, "O that You would tear the heavens apart and come down" (63:19). As soon as Jesus is baptized, the heavens are torn apart. God is breaking into human affairs. The voice speaking to Jesus is that of God confirming for us, the audience, the fundamental title that Mark has given to Jesus.

In showing that the mission of John the Baptist fulfills prophecy, Mark mentions only Isaiah, but his quotation is an amalgamation of texts from two prophets. The first phrase is from the prophet Malachi. The rest, beginning "a voice is crying . . ." is from Isaiah. Such amalgamating of texts was common practice. In addition, Mark *alters* the text of Isaiah. Where Isaiah has "the paths of our God," Mark has simply "his paths." Thus, Mark is identifying Jesus with "the Lord" spoken of in the first of these two parallel sayings, for John's mission is to prepare the way for the Lord, the way for Jesus.

As well as presenting Jesus, the prologue presents also his chief antagonist, Satan. Demons will appear frequently as the story develops, and yet they will *not* prove to be Jesus' greatest adversaries.

In this segment, and in the rest of chapter 1, mark the occurrence of phrases such as "immediately," "at once," "straightaway." They are translations of one Greek word, *euthys*. This word, recurring with the constancy of a drum beat, gives to chapter 1 a sense of swift movement; and that feeling of being constantly on the

move will continue to the end of Mark's story. There is hardly
ever a pause for breath.

Contrasts are made. By his dress and diet, John is identified
with the prophet Elijah (see 2 Kgs 1:8). After the Transfiguration
(9:13) Jesus will confirm this identification. The prophet Malachi
had raised the expectation that Elijah would return to prepare for
the promised Messiah. This is precisely John's role: to prepare for
Jesus. John himself makes the contrast, "I have baptized you with
water, but he will baptize you with the Holy Spirit."

Galilee and Jerusalem

Another important contrast is made here. "The whole Judean
countryside and all the people of Jerusalem" are set against Jesus'
coming from "Nazareth in Galilee." The Jewish Christians in
Rome saw Jerusalem as home. For Mark, Jerusalem and Galilee are
more than geographical areas; they are symbols. Jerusalem was
the center of Jewish orthodoxy. It is the place where one can be at
home as a Jew. With its Temple and priesthood and sacrifices and
Sanhedrin, it is the symbol of everything Jewish. But it is also the
focus of opposition to Jesus. On the other hand, Galilee, with its
cosmopolitan population of Jews and Gentiles, is much more the
mess of real life: Jewish, but rubbing shoulders with—and so
tested by—the world outside Judaism. To the orthodox, Galilee was
suspect. Jerusalem is assuredness; Galilee is ambiguity. Yet Galilee
is where Jesus comes from, and it is to Galilee that he returns, to
set out to establish God's reign. There is an openness about
Galilee; Jerusalem is closed. Jesus does no works of power in
Jerusalem.

In v. 7, "More powerful than I am" is not reminiscent of any
description or expectation about the coming Messiah. Mark
employs it here to prepare for what Jesus will say later (3:27).

The Spirit is described as descending "like a dove." In Gn 1:1–2,
the Spirit of God hovers (like a bird) over the chaos of waters, the
deep. The Babylonian Talmud (Talmud is a collection of ancient
Jewish postbiblical writings) identifies this bird as a dove. The
Babylonian Talmud is a much later writing than any of the New

Testament books, but it may reflect a much earlier tradition. If so, then Mark is evoking, as he does in the title, God's beginning again the work of creation. On the other hand, the dove may also be a symbol of peace, as in the story of Noah's ark. Given the violence of the Spirit immediately afterwards, this is likely to be Mark's intention. Mark likes to jolt. Quite possibly, Mark intends to evoke both meanings, the Spirit of creation and the dove of Noah's ark.

In v. 11 the address to Jesus, "You are my Son, the beloved. With you I am well pleased," is an amalgam of three Old Testament passages: Is 42:1, which begins one of the Servant of God songs; Gn 22:2, which is about the sacrifice of Isaac; and Psalm 2, which was written for the kings' coronation ritual. Thus Mark deftly weaves together several important themes.

Before Jesus returns to that testing world, he must first be tested by the ancient enemy. Readers of Mark are often puzzled by the predominance of exorcisms among Jesus' works of power. They are a continuation of this cosmic episode in the wilderness. The Spirit, Jesus' protagonist, drives him (the Greek means "throw," as in throwing a ball) into the wilderness. With the words *wilderness, testing,* and *forty* Mark deftly evokes the desert experience of God's people, with all of its ambiguity. By the phrase "with the wild beasts," Mark evokes both paradise and the recent scenes in Nero's circus. By the phrase "angels waited on him," Mark reminds them that many of their fellow Christians had died, meaninglessly it would seem, torn to pieces by wild beasts; yet they had persevered, faithful and brave. God had not deserted them.

Excursus 2
Jesus' Divine Sonship

From God's speaking to Jesus, "You are my beloved son," it might be argued that Jesus became, that is, was adopted as, God's son at the baptism. While the argument has some plausibility when taken alone, there is no sense throughout Mark's story that Jesus saw his relationship with

God as adoptive. If Mark had intended an adoptionist meaning—so that Jesus is God's Son not of any innate reality but by adoption—he could easily have made that explicit simply by quoting Psalm 2 more fully: "You are my son; *today* I have begotten you." Mark cannot have God here telling all and sundry who Jesus is (as Matthew does), for the climax of the Gospel comes in the moment after Jesus' death, when, for the first time in the narrative, a human being recognizes who Jesus is. There could not be this climactic moment of recognition if Jesus' identity were made public from the start. Mark's purpose is to have God confirm for Mark's audience the identity that Mark claims for Jesus in the Gospel's title.

However, it is not possible to state clearly and exactly what Mark understands by "the Son of God." There is nothing in Mark's Gospel to suggest that he sees Jesus simply as a man with godlike powers, so that "the Son of God" becomes merely an honorific title. Besides, Mark does not see Jesus' works of power as establishing his uniqueness. Frank Matera and Eduard Schweizer, both modern scholars, see "Son of God" as a unique title in Mark.[4] E. Lohmeyer says, "The Son of God is not primarily a human but a Divine figure. . . . He is not merely endowed with the power of God, but is himself Divine as to his Nature. Not only are his words and works Divine, but his nature is also."[5] I think that Lohmeyer is saying more than can be fairly supposed about Mark's thought-world. Similarly, Vincent Taylor's opinion (great scholar though Taylor is) has few who would support it without any qualification. The Fourth Gospel has seen that if Jesus is divine then he must have preexisted. Mark does not appear to have thought back that far. Neither Mark nor any of the other New Testament authors should be thought of as possessing all the answers to question "What does it mean to call Jesus God?" Nearly two centuries would elapse before the questions that the early ecumenical councils had to address, began to be expressed precisely.

I cannot agree, however, with those authors who present Mark's Christology as a low Christology, so that Mark's Jesus is simply "a son of God." For a while, some scholars thought that the New Testament's understanding of Jesus as divine could be explained by the concept *Theios Anēr*, a demi-god or man with godlike powers. Mention was sometimes made of a certain Apollonius of Tyana, who was said to have performed miracles very similar to those of Jesus. There are supposed to have been many such people in the first century; however, more recent research indicates that the concept *Theios Anēr did not exist* in the first century. In regard to Apollonius, he lived about the same time as Jesus. His life story was written about 200 C.E. by the renowned rhetorician

Philostratus at the behest of Domna Julia, wife of the emperor Septimius Severus. Her purpose was to revive paganism. The biography did lead to a short-lived revival. At that time, the Gospels were all quite public. Supposed resemblances between Apollonius and Jesus are easily seen to be borrowings by Philostratus from the Gospels. According to the *Encyclopedia Britannica* (1968), much of the biography of Apollonius is fanciful.

Raymond Brown's *Introduction to New Testament Christology* provides a readable, scholarly, and reliable introduction to the divinity of Jesus as presented in the New Testament.

NOTES

1. Augustine Stock, *The Call to Discipleship,* Good News Studies 1 (Wilmington, Del.: Michael Glazier, 1982), chapter 8.
2. Raymond E. Brown, S.S., *An Introduction to New Testament Christology* (New York/Mahwah, N.J.: Paulist, 1994), 123 n. 184.
3. Vincent Taylor, *The Gospel according to Mark,* Thornapple Commentaries, 2nd ed. (Grand Rapids, Mich.: Baker Book House, 1981).
4. Frank Matera, *What are they saying about Mark?* (New York/Mahwah, NJ: Paulist, 1987), 29–37. Eduard Schweizer, *The Good News according to Mark* (London: SPCK, 1971), 39, 80, 257–58, esp. 356.
5. E. Lohmeyer, *Das Evangelium nach Markus* (Göttingen: Vandenhoeck & Ruprecht, 1937), 10.

CHAPTER 3

GALILEE I
(MARK 1:1–3:6)

THE MINISTRY IN GALILEE BEGINS
(1:14–45)

The Greek *euthys*—"immediately," "as soon as"—continues to pulsate through the rest of chapter 1. Mark thus paints God's sudden and relentless breaking into our world. *Euthys* occurs eleven times in chapter 1. There is about the movement of this chapter a suggestion not so much of a breath of fresh air as of a whirlwind. But there are also danger signals.

Jesus announces the reign of God. He is not simply saying that God's reign is going to be established soon. He is not the forerunner, preparing for the coming reign of God.[1] He is saying that it has arrived, that his mission is to establish the reign of God. The NRSV's translation of 1:15 is slightly ambiguous, and I have altered it.[2] Jesus is announcing that God, who has been gradually revealing his purpose to his people for nearly two thousand years now, is ready to act definitively. There is a condition though: a continuing *metanoia* ("turning," "repentance") is needed. The precondition for God's reign is our allowing God to reign— "repent and believe the Good News."

So the moment of grace, and the moment for choice, has come. When Jesus says "The time is fulfilled," Mark uses not *chronos,* the Greek word for the ordinary passing moments of time, but *chairos,* the moment of opportunity. We are going to have to choose, and we haven't got forever.

31

Summary of Jesus' Ministry in Galilee

[14]Now after John was (arrested) *delivered up,* Jesus came to Galilee, proclaiming the good news of God,[3] [15]and saying, "The time is fulfilled, and the kingdom of God has (come near) *arrived;* repent, and believe in the good news."

Discipleship

[16]As Jesus passed along the **Sea** of Galilee, he saw Simon and his brother Andrew casting a net into the sea—for they were fishermen. [17]And Jesus said to them, **"Follow me and I will make you fish for people."** [18]And immediately they left their nets and followed him. [19]As he went a little farther, he saw James son of Zebedee and his brother John, who were in their boat mending the nets. [20]Immediately he called them; and they left their father Zebedee in the boat with the hired men, and followed him.

The "sea" of Galilee is a small but deep lake. The River Jordan both flows into it at its northern end and out of it at its southern end. Its surface is six hundred feet below sea level. Though it was called a sea in Nm 34:11, in the first century all writers (secular or religious) call it a lake—all, that is, until Mark quite deliberately misnames it. The sea is the dwelling place of demons. It represents Jesus' struggle with the forces of Satan. Several times Jesus will manifest mastery over this "sea."

The calling of the disciples is obviously a stylized account, in that it consists of two exactly parallel episodes. Mark's purpose is to teach us about discipleship. Most striking for us is the immediacy of their response. In addition, we are being taught that we become Jesus' disciples not first by our choice of him but by his choice of us. Disciples used to choose a rabbi (teacher). Here Jesus does the choosing. He calls them not only to be his pupils and learn from him but to share in his work. The call is to a journey of following behind him, a journey from which there will be no graduating.

Mark now, by narrating an absolutely crowded day in Jesus' early ministry, continues the picture of God's kingdom breaking into the world and seeming to carry all before it.

Verses 21–27 form an *inclusion,* a literary structure indicated by the repetition of a thought at the beginning and the end. This repeated thought is to help interpret the material in between. Inclusion was a commonly used literary technique in Mark's time.

Inclusion

²¹They went to Capernaum; and (when) *immediately* the Sabbath came, he entered the synagogue and **taught.** ²²They were astounded at his **teaching,** for he **taught** them as one having **authority,** and not as the scribes. ²³(Just then) *immediately* there was in their synagogue a man with an unclean spirit, ²⁴and he cried out, "What have you to do with us, Jesus of Nazareth? Have you come to destroy us? **I know who you are, the Holy One of God.**" ²⁵But Jesus rebuked him, saying, "**Be silent,** and come out of him!" ²⁶And the unclean spirit, convulsing him and crying with a loud voice, came out of him. ²⁷They were all amazed, and they kept on asking one another, "What is this? A new **teaching**—with **authority!** He commands even the unclean spirits, and they obey him."

Notice that demons have no difficulty in recognizing who Jesus is. Their naming him is an attempt to gain control over him. For his part, Jesus enjoins silence on them. More than Jesus' exercising mastery over them, the command to silence is part of the messianic secret referred to earlier. Until Jesus hangs dead on the cross, the people's understanding of "Holy One of God" cannot but be wrong.

The crowds are enthusiastic about Jesus, a teacher with authority. The inclusion emphasizes this. When we look and see what the teaching is, we find nothing at all. Jesus has not taught. He has exorcised a demon. Why are they enthusiastic then? Mark deliberately leaves us with a question mark. What is their enthusiasm really about? Is it Jesus' teaching? Or is it his works of power? Mark will eventually caution us against reliance on works of power. Jesus will condemn seeking for proof in signs and wonders. The centurion who recognized God's Son, recognized him not in power but in weakness.

²⁸At once his fame began to spread throughout the surrounding region of Galilee.

²⁹As soon as they left **the synagogue,** they entered **the house** of Simon and Andrew, with James and John. ³⁰Now Simon's mother-in-law was in bed with a fever, and they told him about her at once. ³¹He came and **took her by the hand** and lifted her up. Then the fever left her, and she began to serve them.

There is a movement from the synagogue to the house of a disciple (Peter). Mark is probably symbolizing the movement of his community in Rome away from the synagogue into homes, house-churches. This synagogue/house contrast seems to be operative throughout the Gospel.

Jesus' going into a woman's bedroom and taking her by the hand are acts of familiarity forbidden to any man, let alone a holy man. The ability to see what was freeing and genuine in human customs, and what was crippling and stifling, is a trait of Jesus noted in all the Gospels. When Jesus cures her illness, she gets up and waits. Set free to serve—that is God's salvation. The word used to describe Jesus' raising her up from her bed, *egeiro,* is the same word that Mark will use later about Jesus' resurrection. Both are acts of salvation.

³²That evening, at sundown, they brought to him all who were sick or possessed with demons. ³³And the whole city was gathered around the door. ³⁴And he cured many who were sick with various diseases, and cast out many demons; and he would not permit the demons to speak, because they knew him.

³⁵In the morning, while it was still very dark, he got up and went out to a deserted place, and there **he prayed.** ³⁶And Simon and his

companions **hunted** for him. ³⁷When they found him, they said to
him, "**Everyone is searching for you.**" ³⁸He answered, "Let us go
on to the neighboring towns, so that I may proclaim the message
there also; for that is what I came out to do." ³⁹And he went
throughout Galilee, proclaiming the message in their synagogues
and casting out demons.

Verses 32–34 picture feverish activity around Jesus, and he is
caught up in people's needs. The Greek for Jesus' silencing
demons actually says that he "muzzles" them, as one muzzles a
dog. Mark's language has a fine earthiness.

The next verses paint a contrasting picture of quiet solitude.
While the disciples initially are models of how to answer God's
call, Mark now puts a question mark about them too. Jesus rises
very early to pray. The disciples are caught up with the general
enthusiasm. They scent success, and the smell is sweet to them.
Verse 36 says that the disciples came "hunting" for Jesus as one
hunts for wild animals, and as some in Rome had been hunted as
animals in Nero's circus. This is the only use of the word "hunt, as
for an animal" in the whole of the New Testament. Verse 36 marks
the beginning of what will eventually become the apostles' failure.

⁴⁰A leper came to him begging him, and kneeling he said to him,
"If you choose, you can make me clean." ⁴¹Moved with pity,⁴ Jesus
stretched out his hand and touched him, and said to him, "I do
choose. Be made clean!"
⁴²Immediately the leprosy left him, and he was made clean.
⁴³After sternly warning him he sent him away at once, ⁴⁴saying to
him, "See that you say nothing to anyone; but go, show yourself
to the priest, and offer for your cleansing what Moses commanded,
as a testimony to them." ⁴⁵But he went out and began to proclaim
it freely, and to spread the word, **so that Jesus could no longer go
into a town openly,** but stayed out in the country; and people
came to him from every quarter.

Notice that Jesus touches the leper. Fear of contagion was
enough to bring people to avoid all physical contact with lepers.

Imagine *no one* ever touching you! Jesus' touching was motivated by the man's need. It is a further instance of Jesus' inner freedom.

Mark with delicious irony paints the picture of Jesus. By touching the leper, Jesus had himself incurred taboo. His having to stay outside was the fate of lepers. But Mark is not just enjoying the irony: he is making a strong point. If you reach out to the leper, you may become a leper. Among Mark's community, during the pogrom, there may well have been Christians who, by visiting other Christians in jail, drew suspicion on themselves. As a consequence, they may have found other Christians no longer wanting to know them.

All told, Mark thus far has left us with the impression of great enthusiasm as the initial response to God's breaking into our world. However, he has also foreshadowed future concern. Popularity is not one of the marks of the reign of God.

CONFLICT (2:1–3:6)

We have already met one literary technique of those days, inclusion. Mark here uses another literary technique that, though foreign to us, was common and easily recognized in his time. The series of five conflicts we meet here are arranged according to a concentric structure. In common usage, this structure is often referred to as a *chiasm*. When this structure is used, the key point of it is found in the center. The structure is recognizable because its first segment (A) corresponds to its last (A1), its second (B) to its second last (B1), and so on. So the story works toward a central point. That does not prevent the story from working also toward a climax at the end, as happens in this chiasm. There are many instances of chiasm in Mark, so many that some have asserted that the chiasm was Mark's natural way of writing.

The early enthusiasm gives way to this series of conflicts. In the text below, within (C), highlighted and italicized, is the key reason for the conflicts. The new that Jesus has to offer simply cannot be sown onto the old. While that is the key to the question "why this conflict," it is not the climax of the conflict cycle. That

comes at the end. What begins with asking Jesus, in the first conflict episode, escalates into a plot to kill Jesus, in the last episode.
In this series Mark makes a passing observation about conflict
among human beings. Notice how Jesus' opponents don't take
their complaint to where it belongs.

A: Conflict Begins:
Jesus Heals and Forgives (2:1–12)

[1]When he returned to Capernaum after some days, it was reported
that he was at home. [2]So many gathered around that there was no
longer room for them, not even in front of the door; and he was
speaking the word to them. [3]Then some people came, bringing to
him a paralysed man, carried by four of them. [4]And when they
could not bring him to Jesus because of the crowd, they removed
the roof above him; and after having dug through it, they let down
the mat on which the paralytic lay. [5]When Jesus saw their faith, he
said to the paralytic, **"Son, your sins are forgiven."** [6]Now some of
the scribes were sitting there, **questioning in their hearts,** [7]**"Why
does this fellow speak in this way? It is blasphemy! Who can forgive sins but God alone?"** [8]At once Jesus perceived in his spirit
that they were discussing these questions among themselves; and
he said to them, "Why do you raise such questions in your hearts?
[9]Which is easier, to say to the paralytic, 'Your sins are forgiven,' or
to say, 'Stand up and take your mat and walk'? [10]**But so that you
may know that the Son of Man has authority on earth to forgive
sins**"—he said to the paralytic— [11]"I say to you, stand up, take your
mat and go to your home." [12]And he stood up, and immediately
took the mat and went out before all of them; so that they were all
amazed and glorified God, saying, "We have never seen anything
like this!"

"Who can forgive sins but God alone?" These scribes are asking the right question and should, therefore, be on the way to
finding the right answer. They won't though. Jesus' healing the
cripple does not bring them to see.

Notice that they question in their hearts and among themselves, but will not bring their question to Jesus. He has to confront them with their question. His knowing what is in their hearts does not signify that as God's Son, Jesus knew everything. Divine Jesus certainly is—but human, human mind, human brain, human soul. Each of us has had moments of astuteness when we knew what someone was thinking. There is no need to attribute Jesus' reading their hearts to anything more than perspicacity.

The grammar of the awkward statement in v. 10, "But that you may know . . ." may indicate that it is not Jesus speaking, but Mark. The author intrudes for a moment into the story to address his audience. Imagine a stage, and the actor proclaiming the story. Suddenly the author appears from behind the curtain to say to the audience, "This is the implication for you of what he is doing." The title Son of Man first appears in the Gospel in this statement. Later in this series of conflicts (v. 28), there is a similar Son of Man saying that may, like this one, be an intervention by the author. In each case a problem within Mark's community is addressed. "Son of Man" will not appear again in the story until, in the Gospel's linchpin, Jesus begins to use it as his preferred title for describing his destiny. Here the author seems to be speaking to a dispute about whether the church can forgive sins, and specifically, whether it can receive back those who had defected in the persecution. Mark is, then, using "Son of Man" here to describe Jesus risen, at work now in his church. He makes an identity between the Son of Man and the church. When Mark speaks here of forgiving, he uses the present infinitive, which implies a repeated or continuing action.

Notice that the forgiveness takes place within the *house,* which may be for Mark an image of the church. In Rome, as explained earlier, the church gathered in homes.

Notice also that Mark speaks in v. 4 about a *crowd* gathered at the house. The Greek word he uses, *ochlos,* means "the crowd of ordinary people, not including the leading classes." In this episode the crowd's reaction is quite different from that of the scribes. It will continue that way. Almost to the end of the story, the crowd is on Jesus' side; but at his trial they desert him and turn against him.

B: Food: Jesus Eats with Sinners
(2:13–17)

¹³Jesus went out again beside the sea; the whole crowd gathered around him, and he taught them. ¹⁴As he was walking along, he saw Levi son of Alphaeus sitting at the tax booth, and he said to him, "Follow me." And he got up and followed him. ¹⁵And as he sat at dinner in Levi's house, many tax collectors and sinners were also sitting with Jesus and his disciples—for there were many who followed him. ¹⁶When the scribes of the Pharisees saw that he was eating with sinners and tax collectors, **they said to his disciples, "Why does he eat with tax collectors and sinners?"** ¹⁷When Jesus heard this, he said to them, "Those who are well have no need of a physician, but those who are sick; I have come to call not the righteous but sinners."

For the devout Jew, every meal was a religious meal. Through the meal blessing there was fellowship with God. By dining with tax collectors and sinners Jesus was implying that God accepted them. At stake here are two radically different understandings of holiness, goodness. For the Pharisees, holiness meant being separate from all that is tainted or in any way suspect. For Jesus, holiness embraced the bad to lift them up to goodness. For the Pharisee goodness excluded; for Jesus, goodness included. (Not all Pharisees held the views that Jesus rejected. Nevertheless, many did. The Pharisees were never a very numerous group. In Jesus' time there were about six thousand of them. Their influence was much greater than their numbers might suggest. Of all the parties among the Jews in Jesus' time, the Pharisees were in fact the group to which Jesus was closest in his own thinking. Nevertheless he saw the hypocrisy and self-righteousness of many Pharisees as fundamentally at odds with God's covenant love.) Notice that the Pharisees here bring their criticism of Jesus not to him but to his disciples.

The tax collector here is named Levi. In Matthew's Gospel he is named Matthew. It is generally presumed that Matthew and Levi are the same person, but this is problematic. It was quite common for a Palestinian to have a Jewish name and a Roman name—John (J) Mark (R) is an example. But there is no indication that a man would have two Jewish names. Matthew and Levi are both Hebrew names.

C: A Conflict about Fasting: New and Old Cannot Mix (2:18–22)

[18]Now John's disciples and the Pharisees were fasting; and people came and said to him, "Why do John's disciples and the disciples of the Pharisees fast, but your disciples do not fast?" [19]Jesus said to them, "The wedding guests cannot fast while the **bridegroom** is with them, can they? As long as they have the bridegroom with them, they cannot fast. [20]The days will come **when the bridegroom is taken away from them,** and then they will fast on that day. [21]*No one sews a piece of unshrunk cloth on an old cloak; otherwise, the patch pulls away from it, the new from the old, and a worse tear is made.* [22]*And no one puts new wine into old wineskins; otherwise, the wine will burst the skins, and the wine is lost, and so are the skins; but one puts new wine into fresh wineskins.*"

This time the complaint is about Jesus' disciples, but people bring the complaint to Jesus. The covenant required fasting on one day only in the year, Yom Kippur, the Day of Atonement. The complaint, and Jesus' defense of his disciples, leads to the central reflection. Jesus has come to realize that the new wine he brings cannot be poured into the old wineskins, into what an excessive legalism has made of God's covenant. Jesus cannot build God's kingdom out of an Israel with these leaders. He is going to have to begin afresh, finding new foundations for God's people.

The term *bridegroom* is so extraordinary that some commentators have sought to deny that it was part of Mark's Gospel and to assert that it was a later interpolation. Nowhere in the Old Testament or in intertestamental writing (during the period 100 B.C.E. to 100 C.E. Jewish writing flourished), is the Messiah ever spoken of as bridegroom. God, however, is often spoken of as bridegroom. Though in a veiled fashion, Jesus is laying claim to a much greater title than Messiah; he is revealing his identity. By his talking about "the time when the bridegroom will be taken from them," he is identifying himself as the bridegroom. Moreover, this is the first hint from Jesus' lips of his eventual fate.

B1: Food: Sabbath Controversy
in the Context of Eating (2:23–28)

[23]One Sabbath he was going through the grainfields; and as they made their way his disciples began to pluck heads of grain. [24]The Pharisees said **to him, "Look, why are they doing what is not lawful on the Sabbath?"** [25]And he said to them, "Have you never read what David did when he and his companions were hungry and in need of food? [26]He entered the house of God, **when Abiathar was high priest**, and ate the bread of the Presence, which it is not lawful for any but the priests to eat, and he gave some to his companions."[5] [27]Then he said to them, "The Sabbath was made for humankind, and not humankind for the Sabbath; [28]**so the Son of Man is lord even of the Sabbath.**"

Mark gives an illustration of the incompatibility between the new and the old. The Sabbath rest was a gift of God to his people. Indeed, one of the charges leveled by Gentiles against Jews was that of idleness, because they refused to work on one day each week. However, on account of the hedges around the hedges built to protect the law, this gift of God had become an intolerable burden. An expert in the law would have found five separate violations of the Sabbath in this harmless and innocent action of the disciples. Notice that once again the Pharisees do not take their complaint to where it belongs.

Verse 28 employs once more the term Son of Man. It does not support the argument of v. 27; neither does it follow on from that verse. Mark is intervening once again to speak directly to his community. Presumably, Sunday—the Lord's Day—is being established in Rome, and there is controversy about moving away from, and no longer observing, the ancient Sabbath.[6]

A1: Conflict Complete: Jesus Heals on the Sabbath (3:1–6)

[1]Again he entered the synagogue, and a man was there who had a withered hand. [2]**They watched him** to see whether he would cure him on the Sabbath, so that they might accuse him. [3]And he said to the man who had the withered hand, "Come forward." [4]Then he said to them, "Is it lawful to do good or to do harm on the Sabbath, to save life or to kill?" But they were silent. [5]**He looked around at them with anger**; he was grieved at their hardness of heart and said to the man, "Stretch out your hand." He stretched it out, and his hand was restored. [6]The **Pharisees** went out and immediately conspired with the **Herodians** against him, how to destroy him.

This final conflict scene is intense. When, in v. 2, it says "they watched him," sinister intent is implied. Similarly, in v. 5, when it says that Jesus looked around at them, the Greek means that he looked them in the eye, one by one.

Notice the strongly emotive words, "He looked around at them with anger," "grieved." Pharisees and Herodians were unlikely bedfellows. The Pharisees are well enough known. The Herodians were the secular establishment in Galilee, where Herod was Tetrarch. (Technically, "Tetrarch" means ruler of a fourth part. It was a lower title than King. Herod held his authority subject to Rome, but he was not a mere puppet. From an economic point of view, Herod ruled Galilee well.) Mark points out their conspiring together to highlight the opposition to Jesus from the leadership. The scene is summed up well. Jesus, on the Sabbath gives life to a withered hand; and, in consequence, the leadership on the Sabbath plots his destruction. Thus Jesus' endeavor to establish the reign of God is putting his own life under threat.

When Jesus' ministry began, it seemed that he was going to carry all before him. It has become apparent as opposition gathers that establishing God's reign is not going to be easy at all. His attempt to bring that reign about by his preaching is failing. His ministry has barely begun and already Jesus is marked for death. Something is wrong.

NOTES

1. It is well beyond the scope of this book to give a complete elaboration of what the reign of God means. In the sometimes overfertile apocalyptic writing of the first century there is at times the sentiment that this world has become so bad that God is going to have to destroy it and create anew. That is one understanding of God's reign. A more common understanding was that given expression by Jesus' apostles, "Lord, is this the time? Are you going to restore the Kingdom to Israel now?" (Acts 1:6). Jesus' own understanding of the reign of God cannot be completely identified with any of the expectations current at the time.

Readers who wish to grasp Jesus' understanding of the reign of God would do well to examine one by one all of his statements, and especially all of his parables, about God's reign.

2. See Max Zerwick and Mary Grosvenor, *A Grammatical Analysis of the New Testament* (Rome: Biblical Institute Press, 1981), 101.

3. "Now after John was (arrested) *delivered up.*" Mark uses the Greek word *paradidōmi*. While "arrested" is an accurate translation, Mark's word has a fuller meaning. Mark uses the same word about Judas's betrayal. The verb is in the passive voice, and this is an example of what is called the divine passive. John, and later Jesus, is delivered up by God. This does not mean that God betrayed Jesus (or John). It means that while it took place because of the evil designs of men, this was because God allowed it so that through it he might achieve his gracious purpose.

4. Some ancient manuscripts, instead of "**moved with pity**" have "**becoming angry.**" According to one of the guiding rules of textual criticism, the less likely is the more likely. We can explain how a copyist, coming to an unlikely phrase, decides it is a mistake and sets out to correct it with a more likely one. We cannot explain why a copyist would correct a likely phrase by an unlikely one. So quite possibly Mark had here "becoming angry." If so, we have to inquire what would make Jesus angry here? It would seem to be the doubting implied by "If you want to"; see 9:22–23. I have come across another explanation for Jesus' anger that is ingenious and therefore improbable. The ostracizing of lepers was a requirement of Mosaic law. The original purpose of this requirement is

obvious. In the course of time, circumstances having changed, many points of the Mosaic law had been modified. Yet in this matter of leprosy, there had been no abatement of the rigor of the Mosaic law. The reason for this clinging to the rigor of the law is to be found in the dark side of the human heart. The unneeded harshness of what the law had done to the leper is, in this understanding, what caused Jesus' anger.

5. Ahimelech was high priest, not Abiathar, though Abiathar was a more renowned high priest in David's time. It is possible that Mark is in error, or that Mark's source was in error; or it is possible that Jesus was in error. The notion that the man Jesus, who is the eternal Son of God, knew everything, is maintained by very few people now. The salvation of the human race hardly depends on accuracy about these high priests. However, there is also a simpler explanation. Mark's language here is imprecise. He may simply be referring in general to a period of history. Remember that the Bible did not yet have chapters and verses.

6. There are two definite references to Sunday as the Lord's Day in the New Testament (Acts 20:7; Rv 1:10). In addition, in the Lucan and Johannine accounts of the resurrection, strong emphasis is placed on the first day of the week. The Sabbath is never, in the Old Testament, called the Lord's Day. There was a looking forward to the Day of the Lord, the day when God would step in to set things right; but that had nothing to do with the Sabbath.

CHAPTER 4

GALILEE II
(MARK 3:7–6:6a)

IDENTIFICATIONS (3:7–35)

M ark deals with Jesus' ministry in Galilee in three clearly delineated segments. He begins each segment with a summary of Jesus' ministry and follows the summary with an episode about discipleship. There is a development of discipleship from segment to segment. In Galilee I Jesus calls disciples. In Galilee II he chooses the Twelve. In Galilee III he will send them out on mission. We have met so far two literary techniques from antiquity, the inclusion and the concentric structure, more commonly called the chiasm. We will meet soon a favorite Markan technique—the *sandwich*. In a sandwich Mark begins a story and then interrupts it to switch to a second story. When the second story is complete, he returns to complete the first story. The sandwich technique heightens tension within the plot. But whenever Mark uses this technique, his purpose is more than dramatic. The two stories are always interrelated: they speak to one another and the second story sheds light on the first story.

Part 1: Identifications (3:7–35)

If in the whole of the first half of the Gospel the question Who is this man? hovers continually in the background, that question comes forward to center stage in the early part of Galilee II. People are trying to identify Jesus. For his part, Jesus too identifies those who are his disciples—those who belong and those who do not belong. We are introduced to the image of "insiders" and "outsiders." As the Gospel develops, people who appear to be outsiders will be revealed to be insiders, and those who appear to be insiders—even the Twelve whom Jesus named to be insiders—will be revealed to be outsiders.

Summary

[7]Jesus **departed** with his disciples to the sea, and **a great multitude** from Galilee followed him; [8]hearing all that he was doing, they came to him in great numbers from Judea, Jerusalem, Idumea, beyond the Jordan, and the region around Tyre and Sidon. [9]He told his disciples to have a boat ready for him because of the crowd, so that they would not crush him; [10]for he had cured many, so that all who had diseases pressed upon him to touch him. [11]Whenever the unclean spirits saw him, they fell down before him and shouted, **"You are the Son of God!"** [12]But he sternly ordered them not to make him known.[1]

Seeing that his life is being threatened, Jesus sensibly departs. At a deeper level, this implies Jesus' withdrawing from the synagogue. He has just failed in the synagogue. He leaves, and a great multitude of Jews and pagans (Tyre and Sidon were well outside the land of the Jews) gather to him. If the leaders are rejecting him, the crowds are more enthusiastic than ever. Jesus withdraws to the sea. Mark uses Jesus' crossings of the "sea" of Galilee as an image of his breaking new ground. Here, though, it is withdrawing to the sea, with all its threats. The reign of God is more possible there than in the pious, safe synagogue. If Mark exaggerates the size of the crowds, such exaggeration is common in writings of the time. (The French retain that kind of hyperbole in their phrase *tout le monde*, "the whole world, everybody.")

Earlier, a demon had named Jesus "the holy one of God." Now the demons name him fully, "the Son of God." Their naming Jesus is once again an attempt to gain power over him. This is an understanding of the power of a name that we no longer possess.

Discipleship

¹³He went up **the mountain** and called to him **those whom he wanted,** and they came to him. ¹⁴And he appointed **twelve,** (whom he also named **apostles**),² **to be with him,** and **to be sent out** to proclaim the message, ¹⁵and to have authority **to cast out demons.** ¹⁶So he appointed the Twelve: Simon (to whom he gave the name Peter); ¹⁷James son of Zebedee and John the brother of James (to whom he gave the name Boanerges, that is, Sons of Thunder);³ ¹⁸and Andrew, and Philip, and Bartholomew, and Matthew, and Thomas, and James son of Alphaeus, and Thaddaeus, and Simon the Cananaean, ¹⁹ᵃand Judas Iscariot, who betrayed him.

In v. 13 Jesus calls disciples to him. The call he gave earlier to the four, and then to Levi, he now extends to others. Then, in v. 14, from among those he has called he "makes" the Twelve. Mark uses here a word that is much stronger than "calls." It clearly suggests that he is creating something new. He is beginning a new family or, as we would say, a new people of God. Jesus knows that he is not going to be able to found God's reign on the present leadership among the Jews. The repeated attacks he has already endured make that very clear to him. The new wine cannot be poured into the old wineskins. He must begin a new people. Hence, the creating of the Twelve is not a random choice. They are to be the foundations of the new Israel, as the twelve patriarchs were the foundations of the old Israel.⁴ Given that significance, "the mountain" is meant to evoke Mount Sinai, the place where the old covenant was formed.

Mark lists Jesus' sharing his mission with them. They are to be with him. They are to be sent out to proclaim the Good News—that is, to preach (but not to *teach*)—and to drive out demons. Mark sometimes refers to Jesus himself as preaching the Good News, but more often (thirty times) he speaks of Jesus teaching. "Teacher" is the title that Mark's Jesus is most frequently given. Later we will come to an episode in which the apostles take upon themselves the mantle of teacher.

Jesus has picked out these twelve foundation stones. One, Mark notes, will betray Jesus. As the story develops, it will become obvious that Jesus' choice has been less than perfect.

SANDWICH

Story 1: Jesus' Relatives Identify Jesus

^{19b}Then he went home; ²⁰and the crowd came together again, **so that they could not even eat.** ²¹When **his family** heard it, they went out to restrain him, for (people) *they* were saying, **"He has gone out of his mind."**

Jesus' family members, that is, relatives, have the measure of Jesus; they have made a satisfactory diagnosis: "He has gone mad." The NRSV conveys the impression that other people, not his *relatives,* were saying this. It is possible to read the text that way, but most translators take it to mean his relatives. Because his family reappears in the second part of the sandwich, this is more likely.

Note the reason Mark gives for this judgment: "they could not even eat." This phrase will recur in a similar context.

Story 2: Some Scribes from Jerusalem Identify Jesus, and He Identifies Them

²²And the **scribes** who came down **from Jerusalem** said, "He has Beelzebul, and **by the ruler of the demons he casts out demons."** ²³And he called them to him, and spoke to them in parables, "How can Satan cast out Satan? ²⁴If a kingdom is divided against itself, that kingdom cannot stand. ²⁵And if a house is divided against itself, that house will not be able to stand. ²⁶And if Satan has risen up against himself and is divided, he cannot stand, but his end has come. ²⁷But no one can enter a strong man's house and plunder his property **without first tying up the strong man**; then indeed the house can be plundered. ²⁸"Truly I tell you, people will be forgiven for their sins and whatever blasphemies they utter; ²⁹but **whoever blasphemes against the Holy Spirit can never have for-**

giveness, but is guilty of an eternal sin"—[30]for they had said, "He has an unclean spirit."

These scribes are from Jerusalem. Mark for the first time identifies Jerusalem as the source of opposition to Jesus. Earlier, Jesus had met opposition from Pharisees, and many of the scribes were Pharisees. The Pharisees were neither popular nor influential in Galilee. The ordinary people of Galilee, "the crowd," were religious enough, but they found the Pharisees' nit-picking altogether too much. For their part, the Pharisees referred to the Galilean peasants contemptuously as "the people of the land."

The opinion of Jesus' relatives and friends in Nazareth was bad enough. The identification by which these scribes label Jesus—an agent of the devil—is far worse.[5] Jesus passes judgment on them, which is also a warning. By calling him evil, they are guilty of an eternal sin. In saying that Jesus has an unclean spirit, they have blasphemed against the Holy Spirit. For his part, Jesus in calling Satan the strong man is implicitly calling himself the stronger one to whom John the Baptist had referred (1:7).

Story 1 Completed: Jesus Calls His Relatives Outsiders and Identifies His True Relatives

[31]Then **his mother** and **his brothers** came; and standing **outside,** they sent to him and called him. [32]A crowd was sitting around him; and they said to him, "Your mother and your brothers and sisters are **outside,** asking for you." [33]And he replied, "Who are my mother and my brothers?" [34]And looking at **those who sat around him,** he said, **"Here are my mother and my brothers!** [35]Whoever does the will of God is my brother and sister and mother."

In this, the first of Mark's sandwiches, the interconnection between the two stories is precisely the making of identifications. In the completion of story 1 Jesus makes some identifications of his own. Mark introduces here the differentiation: some people are insiders, and the rest are outsiders. The disciples, those sitting at Jesus' feet (students are still referred to as sitting at their master's feet) are insiders. Jesus' mother and brothers and sisters are outsiders. It is not flesh but faith that makes us belong to Jesus. His family can be universal. (Notice that while Jesus speaks of disciples as being mother and sister and brother, he does *not* include father. Only One is Father to him.)

In this segment of the Gospel, lines of demarcation have been established. The conflict is developing.

Parables (4:1–34)

Concentric Structure (Chiasm)

A: Introduction (and Link to Previous Passage) (4:1–2a)

¹Again he began to teach beside the sea. Such a very large crowd gathered around him that he got into a boat on the sea and sat there, while the whole crowd was beside the sea on the land. ²He began to teach them many things in parables, and in his teaching he said to them:

B: Parable Material (4:2b–20)

Parable of the sower. ³"Listen! A sower went out to sow. ⁴And as he sowed, some seed fell on the path, and the birds came and ate it up.⁶ ⁵Other seed fell on rocky ground, where it did not have much soil, and it sprang up quickly, since it had no depth of soil. ⁶and when the sun rose, it was scorched; and since it had no root, it withered away. ⁷Other seed fell among thorns, and the thorns grew up and choked it, and it yielded no grain. ⁸Other seed fell into good soil and brought forth grain, growing up and increasing and yielding thirty and sixty and a hundredfold." ⁹And he said, "Let anyone with ears to hear listen!"

Interlude: Why Jesus speaks in parables. ¹⁰When he was alone, those who were around him along with the Twelve asked him about the parables. ¹¹And he said to them, "To you has been given the secret of the kingdom of God, but for those outside, everything comes in parables; ¹²in order that 'they may indeed look, but not perceive, and may indeed listen, but not understand; so that they may not turn again and be forgiven.'" [13]And he said to them, "Do you not understand this parable? Then how will you understand (all) *any of* the parables?"

Parable of the sower allegorized and explained. [14]The sower sows the word. [15]These are the ones on the path where the word is sown: when they hear, Satan immediately comes and takes away the word that is sown in them. [16]And these are the ones sown on rocky ground: when they hear the word, they immediately receive it with joy. [17]But they have no root, and endure only for a while; then, when trouble **or persecution** arises on account of the word, immediately they fall away. [18]And others are those sown among the thorns: these are the ones who hear the word, [19]but the cares of the world, and the lure of wealth, and the desire for other things come in and choke the word, and it yields nothing. [20]And these are the ones sown on the good soil: they hear the word and accept it and bear fruit, thirty and sixty and a hundredfold."

C: Sayings Material (4:21–25)

Interlude: (a) The lamp will give light. [21] He said to them, "(Is a lamp brought in) **Does the lamp enter** to be put under the bushel basket, or under the bed, and not on the lampstand? [22]For there is nothing hidden, except to be disclosed; nor is anything secret, except to come to light. [23]Let anyone with ears to hear listen!"

Interlude: (b) This is serious. Don't waste opportunities. [24]And he said to them, "Pay attention to what you hear; the measure you give will be the measure you get, and still more will be given you. [25]For to those who have, more will be given; and from those who have nothing, even what they have will be taken away."

B1: Parable Material (4:26–32)

Two other seed parables. [26]He also said, "The kingdom of God is as if someone would scatter seed on the ground, [27]and would sleep and rise night and day, and the seed would sprout and grow, he does not know how. [28]The earth produces of itself, first the stalk, then the head, then the full grain in the head. [29]But when the grain is ripe, at once he goes in with his sickle, because the harvest has come."

[30]He also said, "With what can we compare the kingdom of God, or what parable will we use for it? [31]It is like a mustard seed, which, when sown upon the ground, is the smallest of all the seeds on earth; [32]yet when it is sown it grows up and becomes the greatest of all shrubs, and puts forth large branches, so that the birds of the air can make nests in its shade."

A1: Conclusion (4:33–34)

Concluding interlude: Why Jesus speaks in parables. [33]With many such parables he spoke the word to them, as they were able to hear it; [34]he did not speak to them except in parables, but he explained everything in private to his disciples.

I think that in the ministry of Jesus, these parables arose out of his grappling with his failure. My understanding of Jesus is that he, God the Son made human, with a human body, a human soul, a human heart, a human mind, a human brain, with all the limitations that implies, set out to establish God's reign. He thought that he could convince people to accept the rule of God. Confronted with shallow enthusiasm at best, and lethal hatred at worst, he realized that he was failing. Out of wrestling with his failure, he came to understand that the songs in Isaiah about a servant of God who would suffer, and passages in Daniel about the faithful son of man who would suffer, were about himself. Trusting his Father, he realized that he had to continue faithfully on a course that would mean rejection for him; but out of that rejection, God would achieve his purpose. Jesus the man was going to have to empty himself in living the commitment to his Father that is the reign of God. Quite certainly, Mark's Gospel presents Jesus as endeavoring to establish the reign of God, and as failing in this endeavor.

Mark's section of parables expresses Jesus' grappling with his failure. In examining the passage, it is important to ask, Why has Mark suddenly introduced this section of parables? There have been no parables hitherto, and only incidental teaching. Why this section? There are three parable stories. There is also an explanation of the first story (which scholars, having studied it in great detail, are convinced did not come from Jesus but was devised by an early Christian community). Each story is about seed that seems to be wasted, getting nowhere. Yet in the end there is outstanding success. Mark has already presented Jesus as, after starting strongly, heading for failure. The parable stories say that the end will not be failure.

This interpretation of Mark's underlying message, the story beneath the story, is reinforced if v. 21 is translated literally; "Does the lamp enter to be put under a bed or under a tub?" Because Mark's Greek is presumed here to reflect an underlying Aramaic mode of expression, v. 21 is translated into the passive voice. The context of it, seed that seems to be failing but in the end will succeed, makes the literal translation of the verse sensible. If the lamp is walking in, it is a person. If a person, who? The answer can only be Jesus himself. Joanna Dewey has argued convincingly that the whole parable section has a concentric structure.[7] Though her work dealt mainly with the first Markan chiasm, she also instanced some of Mark's other chiasms so as to demonstrate that Mark 2:1–3:6 was Mark's own construction and not something he had simply imported from some previous writing. Verse 21 begins the central segment and so is the key to understanding the whole parables segment.

The setting is the Sea of Galilee. Mark, taken literally, has Jesus sitting "on the sea." He is asserting Jesus' power over the evil forces that inhabit the deep. Notice that the parable of the sower does *not* begin "the kingdom of heaven is like. . . ." As Jesus spoke this riddle, the crowd's first reaction would be, "This sower is mad." Peasant farmers in Galilee knew their land well. They would husband the precious seed, not scatter it where it cannot grow. As the story moved to completion, they would think, "this is impossible." Even in ideal conditions, the harvest never yielded thirtyfold, let alone sixty or a hundred. The parable puzzles, as it is meant to. The seed seems to be wasted through prodigal carelessness; but in the end, it is the harvest that is prodigal. What does it mean? Who is the sower? Is it Jesus? Or is it his Father? The explanation of the parable (vv. 13–20) identifies the seed as the word. Jesus, then, is the sower. The explanation does not need further explanation, but the phrase "trouble or persecution on account of the word" should be noted. It indicates that, in Nero's persecution, some did fall away. The faith of some in the community in Rome was superficial.

The other two parable stories, the seed growing while the farmer sleeps and the mustard seed, like the parable of the sower say that in the end the word will be successful. They are explicitly parables about the reign of God. Nothing seems to be happening, but God will see to it that it is fruitful. It seems tiny and insignificant, but it will become large and mighty.

Mark breaks up the parables with interludes. These interludes, if we omit vv. 21–22, are interrelated. The first interlude causes difficulty:

When he was **alone, those who were around him along with the Twelve** asked him about the parables. And he said to them, "**To you** has been given the secret of the kingdom of God, but **for those outside**, everything comes in parables; in order that **they may indeed look, but not perceive**, and may indeed listen, but not understand; **so that they may not turn again and be forgiven**." And he said to them, "**Do you not understand** this parable? Then how will you understand all the parables?"

There is a problem. Jesus was sitting on a boat out on the lake. Now with no intervening change he is alone with his disciples. Chronologically, it is impossible. That is a problem for the fundamentalist in me, but there is a greater problem. Jesus makes a distinction between insiders and outsiders. The disciples are insiders; the members of the crowd are outsiders. The insiders can understand; the outsiders cannot. But it turns out that the insiders cannot understand either. Mark, in fact, is going to continue to probe us as insiders become outsiders, and outsiders become insiders. His whole Gospel and its central character take on the form of a riddle, a parable. Mark, through this device of insiders and outsiders changing places, is attacking smugness and self-righteousness among his Roman Christians.

There is in this segment another, more serious problem: it is the apparent meaning of the phrase "they may look indeed, but not perceive . . . so that they may not turn again and be forgiven." Mark is quoting Is 6:9–10. It seems to mean that Jesus is using parables to keep people from finding salvation. It looks like predestination; that is, it seems to say that Jesus deliberately prevents them from understanding. The problem results from a difference in thinking between the Jew of antiquity and ourselves. There is a passage in Exodus (4:21) which says that God *hardened* pharaoh's heart. Further on (Ex 8:15) it says that pharaoh hardened his heart. For the Semite, the same thought is being expressed in two different ways. Pharaoh hardened his heart—but only because God allowed him to. It all happens within God's sovereignty, within God's providence. We make a distinction between God permitting something to happen (pharaoh hardening his heart) and God positively willing something to happen. The Semites of antiquity did not make this distinction; nor did they find it a problem. The four evangelists and Paul made use of this passage from Isaiah as they wrestled to understand why the majority of God's chosen people had not accepted God's Messiah.

To his community in Rome, and to us, who ask, "Where in all this unholy mess is the reign of God?" these parables of Jesus say, "Trust God! God's reign is growing."

The second interlude—"and he said to them, pay attention to what you hear"—is a warning to insiders to live up to the gift bestowed on them. The warning is occasioned by Jesus' surprise that the disciples do not understand the parable of the sower. Largeness of heart is the determining factor separating insiders from outsiders. If the disciples cannot think big-heartedly, they will lose God's gift to them.

The third interlude (or "postlude," since it concludes the segment)—"With many such parables he spoke the word to them, as they were able to hear it"—is a continuation of the first interlude and a qualifier. In no sense are parables meant to blind; they are to lead toward light.

MIRACLES OF GREAT POWER (4:35–6:6a)

In Galilee I Jesus' miracles or, to be faithful to Mark, his works of power were diffuse, unfocused. Here they are intensely focused; but the overall movement of this segment, the story under the stories, can go unnoticed in the richness of meaning each of these episodes contains. The power of God is seen in Jesus—power over the sea, power over demons, power over sickness, power over death itself. Then, confronted with hearts that are hardened, Jesus, the Son of God, becomes powerless; and Mark ends Galilee II, like Galilee I, with failure.

Power over Nature:
Lord of the Storm and the Sea

³⁵On that day, when evening had come, he said to them, "Let us go across to the other side." ³⁶And leaving the crowd behind, they took him with them in the boat, just as he was. Other boats were with him. ³⁷A great windstorm arose, and the waves beat into the boat, so that the boat was already being swamped. ³⁸But **he was in the stern, asleep on the cushion**; and they woke him up and said to him, **"Teacher, do you not care that we are perishing?"** ³⁹He woke up and rebuked the wind, and said to the sea, "Peace! Be (still) *muzzled!*" Then **the wind ceased, and there was a dead calm.** ⁴⁰He said to them, **"Why are you afraid? Have you still no faith?"** ⁴¹(And they were filled with great awe) *But they became even more afraid* and said to one another, **"Who then is this, that even the wind and the sea obey him?"**

The lake of Galilee, surrounded by hills, is subject to such sudden storms. Mark still calls the lake the sea, because the sea is the dwelling place of death, of the enemy. God, as is narrated in the book of Exodus, by dividing the Red Sea in two had proved himself master of the sea and all that it holds. Thus, the Old Testament, especially the book of Psalms, speaks of God as being Lord of the Sea, Lord of the Storm, Lord of the Wind. Here Jesus shows that lordship. Do the disciples come to see? They are simply left wondering. They have seen Jesus act many times now with the power of God; but they have not come to faith. Their very crying out to him causes him to say "Have you still no faith?" Jesus is baffled by their fear. But even his calming the storm, far from bringing calm to their souls, makes them more afraid still. The cry to Jesus, "Do you not care, we are perishing?" and the picture of Jesus as the pilot of the boat (the cushion at the stern was for the navigator) fast asleep are a vivid reminder to Mark's community of their thoughts and shouts of anguish during the persecution. No doubt each one of us has known of times in our lives when we have thought Jesus asleep and have cried out in agony. The antiphon for the Benedictus on the twelfth Sunday of Year B when this Gospel is read expresses well that the cry of the apostles is the perpetual cry of the little community of Jesus' disciples: "Save us, Lord, we are in peril; speak, God, and there will be peace." (The Benedictus or Canticle of Zachary forms part of the church's prayer each morning.)

On the other hand, the picture Mark gives us of Jesus, sleeping peacefully while the wind and storm raged, suggests that Jesus was possessed of a deep tranquillity.

Power over Demons

¹They came to the other side of the sea, **to the country of the Gerasenes.**[8] ²And when he had stepped out of the boat, immediately a man out of the tombs with an unclean spirit met him. ³He lived among the tombs; and no one could restrain him any more, even with a chain; ⁴for he had often been restrained with shackles and chains, but the chains he wrenched apart, and the shackles he broke in pieces; and no one had the strength to subdue him. ⁵Night and day among the tombs and on the mountains he was always howling and bruising himself with stones. ⁶When he saw Jesus from a distance, he ran and bowed down before him; ⁷and he shouted at the top of his voice, **"What have you to do with me, Jesus, Son of the Most High God? I adjure you by God, do not**

torment me." [8]For he had said to him, "Come out of the man, you unclean spirit!" [9]Then Jesus asked him, "What is your name?" He replied, "My name is Legion; for we are many." [10]He begged him earnestly not to send them out of the country. [11]Now there on the hillside **a great herd of swine was feeding**; [12]and the unclean spirits begged him, "Send us into the swine; let us enter them." [13]So he gave them permission. And the unclean spirits came out and entered the swine; and the herd, numbering about two thousand, rushed down the steep bank into the sea, and were drowned in the sea. [14]The swineherds ran off and told it in the city and in the country. Then people came to see what it was that had happened. [15]They came to Jesus and saw the demoniac sitting there, clothed and in his right mind, the very man who had had the legion; **and they were afraid**. [16]Those who had seen what had happened to the demoniac and to the swine reported it. [17]Then they began to beg Jesus to leave their neighborhood. [18]As he was getting into the boat, **the man who had been possessed by demons begged him that he might be with him**. [19]But Jesus refused, and said to him, "**Go** home to your friends, and **tell** them **how much the Lord has done for you**, and what mercy he has shown you." [20]And he went away and began to proclaim in the Decapolis **how much Jesus had done for him**; and everyone was amazed.

This is one of many episodes that Mark describes so vividly that they read like eyewitness accounts. Mark may *possibly* have been an eyewitness, of course, but he may simply be employing his skill as a teller of stories. Indeed, the picture Mark paints of this man, of his being possessed, is so strong that Mark appears to be making that man a symbol of the whole human race held captive by Satan.

Jesus has crossed the lake once more, broken new ground, and is in Gentile territory. A herd of swine would not be found among a community of Jews. The devils name Jesus, "Son of the most high God," and so seek to best him. Notice that they adjure Jesus, that is, they try to put him on oath and command him. But they delude themselves. Jesus successfully orders and permits them. The pagan villagers react with fear. They want Jesus away from there, because of the loss of their swine. They do not recognize God in Jesus' work of power.

The possessed man, by contrast, seeks to be "with Jesus." This is what Jesus called the Twelve to be. Jesus does not allow it; but he calls the man to be his apostle. "Go home and proclaim what **the Lord** has done for you." This man is an outsider who proves to be an insider. A man who had been horribly possessed becomes the *first* to proclaim Jesus: "He proclaimed through the Decapolis how much **Jesus** had done for him."[9]

SANDWICH

The remaining two manifestations of power are intertwined and form a sandwich. As with all of his sandwiches, Mark interrelates the two events. In this sandwich the woman had the illness for *twelve* years, and the girl is *twelve* years old. This interconnection is too superficial to be Mark's intent. Some suggest that *twelve* symbolizes the old covenant, unable to give health or life, akin to Paul's seeming dismissal of the old covenant in his letter to the Galatians. Mark's remarks about the woman getting worse under the care of physicians lends support to this interpretation. I suggest that Mark's intention is less nasty and more subtle. The woman has an issue of blood (presumably a menstrual flow, which was thought to be blood). Because blood means life, it is sacred, and the woman is taboo. Because she has touched Jesus, Jesus is taboo; Mark's narrative makes her touching of Jesus very public. Because of the taboo, the synagogue ruler would normally have kept his distance from Jesus. But his own daughter's life is at stake. That being the case, he puts the law in its right place.

Story 1 Begins: The Synagogue Ruler's Sick Daughter

[21]When Jesus had crossed again in the boat to the other side, a great crowd gathered around him; and he was by the sea. [22]Then one of the leaders of the synagogue named Jairus came and, when he saw him, **fell at his feet** [23]and begged him repeatedly, "My little

daughter is at the point of death. Come and lay your hands on her, so that she may be made well, and live." ²⁴So he went with him.

Story 2: Power over Sickness

And a large crowd followed him and pressed in on him. ²⁵Now there was a woman who had been suffering from hemorrhages for **twelve years.** ²⁶She had endured much under many physicians, and had spent all that she had; and she was no better, **but rather grew worse.** ²⁷She had heard about Jesus, and came up behind him in the crowd and touched his cloak, ²⁸for she said, "If I but touch his clothes, I will be made well." ²⁹Immediately her hemorrhage stopped; and she felt in her body that she was healed of her disease. ³⁰**Immediately aware that power had gone forth from him,** Jesus turned about in the crowd and said, "Who touched my clothes?" ³¹And his disciples said to him, "You see the crowd pressing in on you; how can you say, 'Who touched me?'" ³²He looked all around to see who had done it. ³³But the woman, knowing what had happened to her, came in fear and trembling, fell down before him, and told him the whole truth. ³⁴He said to her, "Daughter, your faith has made you well; go in peace, and be healed of your disease."

The woman's belief in the power of touching the hem of Jesus' cloak and Jesus' awareness that power had gone out of him bespeak a perception of reality that is foreign to us. Notice that the disciples attempt to correct the master. This will not be the last time they do so.

Story 1 Completed: Power over Death

³⁵While he was still speaking, some people came from the leader's house to say, "Your daughter is dead. Why trouble the teacher any further?" ³⁶But overhearing what they said, Jesus said to the leader of the synagogue, "Do not fear, only believe." ³⁷He allowed no one to follow him except Peter, James, and John, the brother of James. ³⁸When they came to the house of the leader of the synagogue, he saw a commotion, people weeping and wailing loudly. ³⁹When he

had entered, he said to them, "Why do you make a commotion and weep? The child is not dead but sleeping." [40]And they laughed at him. Then he put them all outside, and took the child's father and mother and those who were with him, and went in where the child was. [41]He took her by the hand and said to her, "Talitha cum," which means, "Little girl, **get up**!" [42]And immediately the girl **got up** and began to walk about (she was **twelve years** of age). At this they were overcome with amazement. [43]He strictly ordered them that no one should know this, and told them to **give her something to eat.**

Mark here uses for "get up" the word *egeiro,* which means "rise up," the same word that he used for raising Peter's mother-in-law and that will be used about Jesus' resurrection in chapter 16. That, coupled with Jesus' instruction "give her something to eat," evokes the sacraments of Baptism and Eucharist. Either Mark, or some storyteller before him, has woven this sacramental symbolism into the telling of this episode.

Jesus Becomes Powerless

[1]He left that place and came to his hometown, and his disciples followed him. [2]On the Sabbath he began to teach in the synagogue, and many who heard him were astounded. They said, "Where did this man get all this? What is this wisdom that has been given to him? **What deeds of power are being done by his hands!** [3]Is not this **the carpenter, the son of Mary** and brother of James and Joses and Judas and Simon, and are not his sisters here with us?" **And they took offence at him.** [4]Then Jesus said to them, "Prophets are not without honor, except in their hometown, and among their own kin, and in their own house." [5]**And he *could* do no deed of power there**, except that he laid his hands on a few sick people and cured them. [6]And **he was amazed at their unbelief.**

This is the only place in the New Testament where we are told that Jesus was a carpenter. The people of Nazareth, according to

Mark, refer to him also as "the son of Mary." Almost certainly, it
is meant as a slur, implying that Jesus was illegitimate. Given the
kind of town Nazareth was, and the knowledge we have of Jesus'
conception from the Gospel of Luke and especially from the
Gospel of Matthew, the slur is not unexpected.

The rejecting of the prophet in his own country is an unextra-
ordinary manifestation of the "cutting someone down to size"
syndrome. They know Jesus' works of power; like the apostles,
they ask, "Who is he?" But small-town thinking leads them to
reject him, to such an extent that Mark says, "He could do no
deed of power there." It is such a big statement that Mark immediately qualifies it in a way that leaves us confused. Why does
"laying hands on sick people and curing them" not qualify as a
work of power? Mark concludes Galilee II with a most frightening
statement: When faced with the refusal of the human heart, God-
made-one-of-us becomes powerless. Fortunately, later in the
Gospel we will be told that "for God, all things are possible." But
for the moment Jesus, powerless and feeling a sense of failure,
stands there amazed at their lack of faith. At the beginning of the
Gospel, after introducing Jesus, Mark introduced Jesus' opponent,
Satan. But the most difficult opponent is not Satan at all! It is people. Mark will have no truck with any endeavor to transfer the
blame for our hard-heartedness, our refusal to hear, onto the
devil.

EXCURSUS 3

THE PLACE OF MARY IN THE GOSPEL OF MARK

The only references to Mary in the Gospel of Mark are in 3:32 and 6:3.
In chapter 3 Jesus' mother, along with his brothers and sisters, is placed
by Jesus among the outsiders. In addition, in 3:21, Mark probably intends
to include Mary among the relatives who think that Jesus has gone mad.
The very mention of brothers and sisters of Jesus is enough to produce
panic among conservative Catholics like myself. What is going on?

In the first place, it must be said that if Mark's Gospel provided the
only information about Mary in the New Testament, then the scriptures
would provide us with no foundation for a "theology" of Mary, nor for
devotion to her. In the second place, if Rome in 69 C.E. had developed any

sort of appreciation of Mary's role in her Son's work, Mark could not have written about her the way he did. This should not surprise us. God's revelation is complete in Jesus; but our understanding of it is gradual, and the early growth in understanding was uneven from place to place.

Having stated the above, it can easily be understood why Mark includes Mary among the outsiders. His message is "Faith is what matters, not kin." Mark does not see a problem with stating that. Even that message has to be subsumed into the still more important message of Mark: You cannot know Jesus until you look at the cross.

The other problem is that Jesus is said to have brothers and sisters. The words Mark uses ordinarily refer to blood brothers and sisters. They do not *have* to. There are instances in the New Testament of *adelphos* (= blood brother) being used to describe brotherhood in the Christian community, where there is no blood relationship at all. It must also be remembered that Mark's original language is Aramaic, where "brothers and sisters" can embrace a whole clan. In addition, we should not be reading the nuclear family, which for the human race is still a novelty, back into Jesus' family in Nazareth. Jesus would have grown up as one of a "herd" of brothers and sisters in the clan.

In the case of these four brothers mentioned—James and Joses, Simon and Jude—it would appear that blood brotherhood is *not* meant; for in Mark 15:40 James and Joses appear as the sons of a Mary who is *not* the mother of Jesus; for, in the context, if she were Jesus' mother, Mark would have said so. That is as far as we can take it. Mark's Gospel neither proves nor disproves Jesus' having blood brothers and sisters.

NOTES

1. If understood literally, this passage is impossible. The devils are screaming out who Jesus is, yet no one pays any attention to them. Fundamentalism founders on passages like this. Mark's message is what matters. Devils quickly recognize the secret of Jesus, but human beings don't. Nor will Jesus let the devils propagate their knowledge: until Jesus is dead, all knowledge of him falls far too short of the reality of his identity.

2. "Whom he also named apostles" is missing from many manuscripts. Most likely some copyist inserted it into Mark.

3. As usual, when Mark uses an Aramaic word, he translates it. But he offers no reason for this nickname. An episode in Luke (9:51–56) may explain it.

4. As the patriarchs of the twelve tribes of the new people of God, each of the Twelve is, of necessity, male. However, no argument whatsoever supporting the restriction of Christian leadership to males in later times can be adduced from Jesus' choice of males to be the "founding fathers" for his new people.

5. Though Mark speaks of demons, unclean spirits, Satan, and Beelzebul, the word *devil* never appears in the second Gospel. Nevertheless, it is quite clear that Mark (and Mark's Jesus) regards these as personal forces at enmity with God's purpose. The question of whether those afflicted with unclean spirits were really possessed by outside personal forces is not a question Mark was asked. Obviously, then, we should not expect Mark's Gospel to answer the question.

6. Usually we associate the word parable with a story. Parable translates the Hebrew word *mashal,* which means "riddle." A parable can be a story, a symbolic action, or a saying. The essential quality of a parable is that it jolts people, inviting them to ask questions of themselves.

7. Joanna Dewey, *Markan Public Debate: Literary Technique, Concentric Structure, and Theology of Mark 2:1–3:6,* Society of Biblical Literature Dissertation Series 48 (Chico, Calif.: Scholars Press, 1980).

8. Mark's geography is said to be imprecise here. Gadara was about thirty miles from the lake. It is argued that the author of this Gospel cannot therefore be the John Mark from Jerusalem. However, Mark refers to a general area. Besides, there is no reason to presume that a Jerusalemite of those times would know well the geography of northern Palestine. The imprecision does, however, argue against Galilee as the locus of Mark's Gospel.

9. Jesus had told him to proclaim how much *the Lord,* that is *God,* had done for him. The man proclaims how much *Jesus* had done for him. The implicit identification of "Jesus" with "the Lord" does not appear to be accidental. Luke, in narrating this episode will make the identification even more explicit (Lk 8:39).

CHAPTER 5

MARK 6:6b–8:33

GALILEE III: BREAD FOR THE WORLD
(6:6b–8:21)

M ark has used *bread* as a binding motif throughout this last segment of Jesus' ministry in Galilee. I have italicized bread, loaves (the same word in Greek as bread), and fragments to highlight its frequent recurrence. These words occur twenty times in the whole of the Gospel. Of these occurrences, eighteen are in Galilee III. Mark's underlying message is that Jesus is the bread God gives us all. In the previous segment about power, Mark's structure was very logical—mechanical one might say—and certainly easy to follow. Usually his structure is not so simple. Mark is called the "action" Gospel; the story keeps moving swiftly toward its goal. So in these segments, one event leads into the next, and the story advances.

Part 1: God at Work among Us
(6:6b–52)

Galilee III commences with an extremely brief summary. In Galilee I, Jesus began calling disciples. In Galilee II, he chose the Twelve. Now he sends the Twelve out to preach. The episode about Herod and John is to remind us of the dangers of talking repentance. No such danger threatens the apostles though, because they fail to preach repentance.

As with the miracles in Galilee II so here the twin miracles of Jesus' feeding the five thousand and his walking on the sea are extremely focused. They are saying that the God who led his people out of Egypt is now here walking among his people.

Summary

⁶ᵇThen he went about among the villages teaching.

SANDWICH

Story 1 Begins: Discipleship. The Twelve Are Sent Out to Preach Repentance.

⁷He called the Twelve and began to send them out **two by two**, and gave them authority over the unclean spirits. ⁸He ordered them to **take nothing** for their journey except a staff; no *bread*, no bag, **no money** in their belts; ⁹but to wear sandals and not to put on two tunics. ¹⁰He said to them, "Wherever you enter a house, stay there until you leave the place. ¹¹If any place will not welcome you and they refuse to hear you, as you leave, shake off the dust that is on your feet as a testimony against them." ¹²So **they went out and proclaimed that all should repent.** ¹³They cast out many demons, and anointed with oil many who were sick and cured them.

Their being sent out two by two implies that we are never meant to be on our own in Christ's work. Nevertheless, as Mark's story progresses, Jesus himself in his living the Gospel becomes more and more alone. "Take nothing . . . ," they are to depend on God and on the people among whom they preach. It is an enormous, frightening risk that Jesus asks of them. They are to live the trust in God that is fundamental to the acceptance of God's reign; otherwise their preaching will not ring true.

The next segment, about Herod and John the Baptist, provides a time gap between the apostles' going on mission and their return; but it is much more than that. Underlying the whole of the first half of the Gospel is the question: Who is Jesus? Herod's attempt to identify Jesus is pitiable. In a couple of lines, Mark conjures the picture of a fear-crazed tyrant. And yet his picture of Herod is not one of simple reprobation. The word Mark uses about Herod's keeping John the Baptist safe, *syntēreō*, is used only three times in the whole of the New Testament and means "treasured," as in Luke's infancy narrative "Mary treasured all these things and pondered them in her heart." Mark pictures Herod as one who had elements of real greatness in him but who surrendered himself to convenience. Mark here quite deliberately calls Herod Antipas not tetrarch but "king." He is evoking the picture of the king of Persia. In antiquity the title King *(basileus)* was usually reserved for that king. Many elements of Mark's narration of the detailed circumstances of John the Baptist's death at the hands of Herod are unlikely, and Mark's readers would have recognized this. For example, Salome, a princess, would never have danced at the banquet. It would have been absolutely beneath her station. Mark's narrative here borrows a number of phrases from the book of Esther, the story of a Jewish woman married to the king of Persia. Esther interceded with the king for the life of her fellow Jews, quite a contrast to the prayers of Herod's daughter and wife here.[1] It is beyond the scope of this book to examine the story in detail. Suffice it to grasp the main message, the fate of one who preached repentance.

Meanwhile, Mark's audience is left wondering how the Twelve are going to fare in their preaching. Mark mentioned among Jesus' directions to the Twelve that they were to take no money with them. We will find soon that the Twelve either ignored this direction or else enriched themselves along the way.

Story 2: The Fate of One Who Preached Repentance

Herod tries to identify Jesus. **[14]King Herod** heard of it, for Jesus' name had become known. Some were saying, "John the baptizer has been raised from the dead; and for this reason these powers are at work in him." **[15]**But others said, "It is Elijah." And others said, "It is a prophet, like one of the prophets of old." [16]But when Herod heard of it, he said, "**John, whom I beheaded, has been raised.**"

Flashback: The death of John the Baptist. [17]For Herod himself had sent men who arrested John, bound him, and put him in prison on account of Herodias, his brother Philip's wife, because Herod had married her.

[18]For John had been telling Herod, "It is not lawful for you to have your brother's wife." [19]And Herodias had a grudge against him, and wanted to kill him. But she could not, [20]for Herod feared John, knowing that he was a righteous and holy man, and **he protected him**. When he heard him, he was greatly perplexed; and yet he liked to listen to him. [21]But an opportunity came when Herod on his birthday gave a banquet for his courtiers and officers and for the leaders of Galilee. [22]When her daughter Salome came in and danced, she pleased Herod and his guests; and the king said to the girl, "Ask me for whatever you wish, and I will give it." [23]And he solemnly swore to her, "Whatever you ask me, I will give you, even half of my kingdom." [24]She went out and said to her mother, "What should I ask for?" She replied, "The head of John the baptizer." [25]Immediately she rushed back to the king and requested, "I want you to give me at once the head of John the Baptist on a platter." [26]The king was deeply grieved; yet out of regard for his oaths and for the guests, he did not want to refuse her. [27]Immediately the king sent a soldier of the guard with orders to bring John's head. He went and beheaded him in the prison, [28]brought his head on a platter, and gave it to the girl. Then the girl gave it to her mother. [29]**When his disciples heard about it, they came and took his body, and laid it in a tomb.**"

John's death in such circumstances appears meaningless, absurd, the same as the fate of Christians in the persecution of Nero. The fate of one who preached repentance invites the audience to wonder more strongly what the fate of the Twelve will be, to link John's with the fate of Jesus, and to ponder their own vocation. The remark about John's disciples taking his body and burying it invites comparison with the action of the Twelve after Jesus dies.

Story 1 Completed: The Twelve Return

[30]The apostles gathered around Jesus, and told him **all that they had done and taught.** [31]He said to them, "Come away to a deserted place all by yourselves and rest a while." For many were coming and going, and **they had no leisure even to eat.** [32]And they went away in the boat to a deserted place by themselves.

The apostles return from their journey full of themselves. Their reporting to Jesus can be translated accurately "all that *they* had done, and all that *they* had taught."[2] They have been successful; but success has gone to their heads. They think that *they* are driving out devils. Previously they have called Jesus "Teacher" (4:38). Now they are teachers. They have graduated, they think, from discipleship. This is the fundamental failure of the Twelve: they are self-made; they won't let Jesus make them. Not until they have reached rock bottom will Jesus be able to begin to form them as his disciples; although he does set out immediately to do something. Earlier, when Jesus did not have time even to eat (3:20), his relatives, deciding that he was beside himself, set out to take him in charge. Now, when the apostles have no time even to eat, and *are* beside themselves, Jesus sets out to take them in charge, "Come away to a deserted place. . . ." But the crowd frustrates his good purpose. He wants to form the Twelve; he needs to form the Twelve; but the need of the crowd takes over. It is the mess of real life, the divine mess.

EXODUS EVENTS (6:33–52)

This segment needs careful attention. From one point of view the feeding is the first part of an inclusion; there is a second feeding in chapter 7. From another point of view, this completes the discipleship segment. Prevented by the crowd from spending time in forming the Twelve, Jesus makes use of the crowd's very need to teach the Twelve a lesson in discipleship. The Twelve had come back full of themselves. They can drive out devils. They have become teachers. Nothing should be too difficult for them. After

Jesus' day of teaching, they perceive a problem: the people are hungry. They have an answer for the problem too: "Send them away." With delicious irony, Jesus says to these experts, "*You* give them something to eat." Their answer indicates that they have money. They did not set out to preach in the manner Jesus had told them to. Because of Jesus, they *become* able to feed the crowd. However, as Jesus continuously hands out bread to them for the people, the Twelve have to continue coming back to Jesus for that bread. (The Greek verb carries the definite sense of continuing action. Greek verbs have many more tenses than English verbs.) That is the relationship Jesus means for them—depending on him, not on themselves.

In addition, the feeding has a eucharistic aspect. So strongly does it resonate the eucharistic action that the Roman canon, in the words of institution, uses a phrase from here: "Looking up to heaven," which is in none of the New Testament accounts of the Last Supper.

There is a still more important aspect. I have labeled this segment "exodus events." Through the feeding and Jesus' walking on the water, there is a clear message: God who once led his people out of Egypt stands once more among them.

6:33Now many saw them going and recognized them, and they hurried there on foot from all the towns and arrived ahead of them. 34As he went ashore, he saw a great crowd; and **he had compassion for them, because they were like sheep without a shepherd;** and he began to **teach** them many things. 35When it grew late, his disciples came to him and said, "This is a deserted place, and the hour is now very late; 36**send them away** so that they may go into the surrounding country and villages and buy (something) *bread* for themselves to eat." 37But he answered them, **"You give them something to eat."** They said to him, "Are we to **go and buy two hundred denarii worth of** *bread*, and give it to them to eat?" 38And he said to them, "How many *loaves* have you? Go and see." When they had found out, they said, "Five, and two fish." 39Then he ordered them to get all the people to sit down in groups **on the green grass.** 40So they sat down **in groups of hundreds and of**

fifties. [41]Taking the five *loaves* and the two fish, he looked up to heaven, and blessed and broke the *loaves*, and gave them to his disciples to set before the people; and he divided the two fish among them all. [42]And all ate and were filled; [43]and they took up twelve baskets full of (broken pieces) *fragments* and of the fish. [44]Those who had eaten the *loaves* numbered five thousand men. [45]Immediately he made his disciples get into the boat and go on ahead to the other side, to Bethsaida, while he dismissed the crowd. [46]After saying farewell to them, he went up on the mountain to pray.

Mark says that Jesus had compassion for them, for they were like sheep without a shepherd. That line evokes Ezechiel 34. There God, fed up with the dishonesty of Israel's shepherds, made the promise, "I myself will pasture my sheep." Mark further points out that the people are told to sit down on *the green grass.* This is a completely unexpected and seemingly useless detail, except that it evokes Psalm 23. Psalm 23 begins, "The Lord is my shepherd"; and, further on, it says, "He makes me lie down in green pastures." God has come to be his people's shepherd.

Another apparently useless detail makes it clear that the Jews' being fed with manna in the desert is being evoked here. They sit down in groups of *hundreds and fifties.* This is how they traveled through the desert after their escape from Egypt. Mark is not saying here that Jesus is a new Moses, here to set God's people free. Nothing in Mark's Gospel supports that interpretation. He is saying rather, "God is here, shepherding his people, feeding them, leading them."

When we look at the sequel to the feeding, Jesus' walking on the water, Mark's message emerges still more forcefully.

[47]When evening came, the boat was out on the sea, and he was alone on the land. [48]When he saw that they were straining at the oars against an adverse wind, he came towards them early in the morning, walking on the sea. **He intended to pass them by.** [49]But when they saw him walking on the sea, they thought it was a ghost and cried out; [50]for they all saw him and were terrified. But

immediately he spoke to them and said, "(Take heart, it is I;) **Courage! I AM [YAHVĒ] [EGŌ EIMI]. Do not be afraid.**" [51]Then he got into the boat with them and the wind ceased. And **they were utterly astounded,** [52]**for they did not understand about the** *loaves,* **but their hearts were hardened.**

In the previous miracle cycle, it was pointed out that, because of the parting of the Red Sea, God was spoken of as Lord of the Sea.[3] Here, immediately after evoking one exodus event, Mark evokes a further two exodus events. The first is obvious now: Jesus walking on the water is Lord of the Sea. By the phrase "he intended to pass them by," Mark suggests that this event is meant to be seen in the context of the exodus. It calls to mind God's passing by Moses on Mount Sinai. Of much greater import are the words Jesus speaks to the frightened apostles, "Courage! I AM! Do not be afraid!" It was at Mount Sinai that God revealed to Moses his name, if name we should call it, the name we usually write as Yahweh. When Moses asked God his name, so that he might tell his fellow Jews should they ask him, the answer God gave him was "I AM WHO I AM." "Tell them that I AM has sent you." When the Old Testament was first translated into Greek (about 300 B.C.E.) the divine name was translated *"EGO EIMI."* In English, this means "I AM." That is how the Jews understood God's name; and that is what Jesus speaks here. In several Old Testament texts, God speaks to his people in words almost identical to what Mark writes here: Is 41:10: "Do not be afraid, for I am with you; have no fear, I am your God; I will give you strength, I will help you, I will uphold you with my strong right hand." Is 43:5–6: "Do not be afraid, for I am with you; I will gather your offspring . . . from the east, and from the west . . . from the north and the south I will gather you." Jer 46:28: "As for you my servant Jacob, says Yahweh, do not be afraid for I am with you." Almost certainly, Mark is presenting Jesus as using the divine name, and speaking to the Twelve as often God had spoken, "Courage! I AM! Do not be afraid."[4]

Mark almost overloads the description of these twin miracles with evocative details to speak more loudly Jesus' self-revelation, "The God of the Exodus is here among his people."

The people witness only the feeding. The apostles witness the walking on the sea. They hear the words Jesus speaks. Mark points out that they do not understand; and he says sadly of the Twelve what Jesus had seen earlier (3:5) in some Pharisees, "Their hearts were hardened." Once already, when Jesus was asleep in the boat they had encountered the Lord of the Sea. They had not understood then either. No doubt Mark's Roman Christians, once super-confident, had in the persecution been able to empathize with the apostles rowing against the strong wind, feeling that the Lord had passed them by.

THERE IS BREAD LEFT OVER (6:53–8:10)

The emphasis at the end of the feeding on the large quantity of bread left uneaten leads us naturally into this section on breads. There is bread left over because, first, the Pharisees are making it impossible for many Jews to eat, and, second, because the Gentiles are excluded from the table.

Mark opens this segment with a fairly large summary. Following that is a segment involving disciples and Pharisees. Jesus defends his disciples.

Summary (6:53–56)

⁵³When they had crossed over, they came to land at Gennesaret and moored the boat. ⁵⁴When they got out of the boat, people at once recognized him, ⁵⁵and rushed about that whole region and began to bring the sick on mats to wherever they heard he was. ⁵⁶And wherever he went, into villages or cities or farms, they laid the sick in the marketplaces, and begged him that they might touch even the fringe of his cloak; and all who touched it were healed.

The Pharisees Are Making It Impossible
for Many Jews to Eat (7:1–23)

¹Now when the Pharisees and some of the scribes **who had come from Jerusalem** gathered around him, ²they noticed that some of

his disciples were eating *bread* with defiled hands, that is, without washing them. [3](For the Pharisees, and all the Jews, do not eat unless they thoroughly wash their hands, thus observing the tradition of the elders; [4]and they do not eat anything from the market unless they wash it; and there are also many other traditions that they observe, the washing of cups, pots, and bronze kettles.) [5]So the Pharisees and the scribes asked him, "Why do your disciples not live according to the tradition of the elders, but eat *bread* with defiled hands?" [6]He said to them, "Isaiah prophesied rightly about you hypocrites, as it is written, 'This people honors me with their lips, but their hearts are far from me; [7]in vain do they worship me, teaching human precepts as doctrines.' [8]You abandon the commandment of God and hold to human tradition." [9]Then he said to them, "You have a fine way of rejecting the commandment of God in order to keep your tradition! [10]For Moses said, 'Honor your father and your mother'; and, 'Whoever speaks evil of father or mother must surely die.' [11]But you say that if anyone tells father or mother, 'Whatever support you might have had from me is Corban' (that is, an offering to God)— [12]then you no longer permit doing anything for a father or mother, [13]thus making void the word of God through your tradition that you have handed on. And you do many things like this."

[14]Then he called the crowd again and said to them, "Listen to me, all of you, and understand: [15]there is nothing outside a person that by going in can defile, but the things that come out are what defile." [17]When he had left the crowd and entered the house, his disciples asked him about the parable. [18]He said to them, "Then do you also fail to understand? Do you not see that whatever goes into a person from outside cannot defile, [19]since it enters, not the heart but the stomach, and goes out into the sewer?" **(Thus he declared all foods clean.)** [20]And he said, "It is what comes out of a person that defiles. [21]For it is from within, from the human heart, that evil intentions come: fornication, theft, murder, [22]adultery, avarice, wickedness, deceit, licentiousness, envy, slander, pride, folly. [23]All these evil things come from within, and they defile a person."

Notice that Mark once again highlights the opposition to Jesus as coming from Jerusalem.

The requirements about washing and so on were not based on the law of Moses. They were Pharisaic elaborations, oral law meant to put "hedges" around the law so that not even through inadvertence might the law be transgressed. Because we tend mentally to identify Judaism with the Pharisees, it is timely to remember that not all Jews agreed with Pharisaism; and not all Pharisees would have subscribed to the kind of legalism that gave rise to this interpretation of *corban*.

Mark finds it necessary to explain in detail Jewish practices. Some of his Gentile audience were evidently uninformed about Judaism. Others in his audience were rigid adherents to Judaism. At v. 19, Mark steps from behind the curtain again to speak to his audience. His terse words, "Thus he declared all foods clean," are one of the most definite statements in the whole of the New Testament that the Old has been surpassed. At the same time, they provide a strong guarantee that Mark's account of Jesus is in accord with the tradition Rome had received. Some of the Jewish Christians would be seething with rage at this aside of Mark. They would be after Mark's scalp. If Mark were not substantially faithful to the tradition they already had learned, then they would have had him for breakfast. Once again Mark is very clear in this segment and little elaboration is needed. Jesus' concern is about healing; these Pharisees are concerned about washing. Moral goodness is a matter not of ritual taboos but of real goodness, which proceeds from the heart.

The Gentiles Have Been Excluded from the Table (7:24–8:10)

The Syrophoenician Woman

24From there he set out and went away to the region of Tyre. He entered a house and did not want anyone to know he was there. Yet he could not escape notice, 25but a woman whose little daughter had an unclean spirit immediately heard about him, and she came and bowed down at his feet. 26Now the woman was **a Gentile**, of Syrophoenician origin. She begged him to cast the demon out of her daughter. [27]He said to her, "Let the children be fed first, for it is not fair to take the children's (food) *bread* and throw it to the dogs." [28]But she answered him, "Sir, even the dogs under the table eat the children's *crumbs*." [29]Then he said to her, "For saying that, you may go—the demon has left your daughter." [30]So she went home, found the child lying on the bed, and the demon gone.

Mark is not afraid to tell this episode, in which Jesus seems to be unkind. Nor does he resolve it so that we can say that he is not really being unkind at all. We are left trying to think of excuses for Jesus' rudeness toward the Syrophoenician woman. The Jews, in one of those mental gymnastics by which feelings of inferiority are turned into feelings of superiority, had taken to calling the Gentiles dogs. Jesus here appropriates that term. The word Jesus employs carries a diminutive element. It means "puppy dogs" rather than dogs. Perhaps Jesus spoke to the woman with a smile on his face that told her he was "stirring," and that produces her quick-witted rejoinder. Perhaps!—but Mark does not tell us. In fact the apparent rudeness may not have caused concern to Mark's audience. They may have recognized it simply as a battle of wits. The fact that the woman bests Jesus in the argument, however, would have caused Mark's audience both concern and embarrassment. To be beaten in an argument by a woman brought shame on Jesus, and no man would own such a defeat; but Jesus does. In the ancient Mediterranean world (and in the most traditional cultures) *honor*, the opposite of which is shame, is a fundamental value. To force a person into shame is to court revenge. In the West we pretend that honor is unimportant, "I don't care what anyone thinks of me," but we really hold it to be quite important. Self-esteem can't begin without the esteem of others. In the Middle East, the importance of honor is recognized, not denied or concealed. Matters of honor and shame are out in the open. Mark does not conceal Jesus' defeat, and, when the reader's initial shock has passed, it may be noticed that this unique man, Jesus, feels no concern about being bested.

The woman herself steps from nowhere onto center stage for a few moments and elicits from Jesus a change in attitude. She is one of those outsiders to the Gospel story who seem to belong inside, there to warn Mark's audience that all smug self-satisfaction is dangerous. This episode is important for Mark's unique presentation of Jesus, one who, though he is God among us, is very much one of us.

The message of the episode should not be missed. The Gentiles are to receive the children's bread. Jesus has reached out here into definitely pagan territory.[5] He had planned earlier (6:32) to get time alone with his disciples. The crowd of Jews that needed him forced him to postpone their retreat. Now, when Jesus has taken them away well into pagan territory, a pagan intervenes to redirect his plans. Jesus had seen his mission as giving bread to the children of Israel. The woman demands bread for the pagan household pets as well, and Jesus sees that pagans can have the faith that belongs to the children.

Summary of Jesus' Work in Gentile Territory

[31]Then he returned from the region of Tyre, and went by way of Sidon towards the Sea of Galilee, in the region of the Decapolis.

Mark here portrays Jesus going around the pagan areas to the north and east of Galilee. He has proclaimed the gospel in Galilee, and now he reaches out to the Gentiles. Much has been written about the awkwardness of Mark's geography here. Jesus' journey would be something like traveling from Chicago to New York via Denver. From his apparent ignorance of the area it has been argued that Mark could not have been a Palestinian Jew. His geography certainly does argue against the Gospel's having been written in Galilee, but a native of Jerusalem could easily lack detailed knowledge of northern Galilee. Further, Mark may not have been ignorant at all. His purpose here is to portray, as strongly as he may legitimately do it, a mission of Jesus among the Gentiles. It would be natural for him, writing in far-off Rome, to mention better-known places in the region, such as Sidon, the Decapolis.

In Pagan Territory, Jesus Opens a Man's Ears

³²They brought to him a deaf man who had an impediment in his speech; and they begged him to lay his hand on him. ³³He took him aside in private, away from the crowd, and put his fingers into his ears, and **he spat and touched his tongue.** ³⁴Then looking up to heaven, he sighed and said to him, "Ephphatha," that is, "Be opened." ³⁵And immediately his ears were opened, his tongue was released, and he spoke plainly. ³⁶Then Jesus ordered them to tell no one; but the more he ordered them, the more zealously they proclaimed it. ³⁷They were astounded beyond measure, saying, "He has done everything well; he even makes the deaf to hear and the mute to speak."

The episode is symbolic. Jesus opens the ears of a pagan to hear (the Good News). As a result, the pagans once again proclaim (the Good News); and, as previously with the pagan man at Gerasa, the Good News they proclaim is Jesus.

Jesus takes spittle from his mouth and touches the man's tongue. According to Jewish purity laws spittle and all body fluids were unclean.[6] Such laws sprang originally from perceived health requirements. Their perception was not always accurate, but as their perception, it was decisive. Mark, by mentioning in this context Jesus' action, is implying that these purity laws do not hold with the pagans.

Jesus Gives Bread to the Gentiles

¹In those days when there was again a great crowd without anything to eat, he called his disciples and said to them, ²"I have compassion for the crowd, because they have been with me now for three days and have nothing to eat. ³If I send them away hungry to their homes, they will faint on the way—and some of them have come from a great distance." ⁴His disciples replied, "How can one feed these people with *bread* here in the desert?" ⁵He asked them,

"How many *loaves* do you have?" They said, "Seven." [6]Then he ordered the crowd to sit down on the ground; and he took the seven *loaves*, and **after giving thanks** he broke them and gave them to his disciples to distribute; and they distributed them to the crowd. [7]They had also a few small fish; and after blessing them, he ordered that these too should be distributed. [8]They ate and were filled; and they took up the broken (pieces) *fragments* left over, **seven baskets** full. [9]Now there were about four thousand people. And he sent them away. [10]And immediately he got into the boat with his disciples and went to the district of Dalmanutha.

Jesus has gone among the Gentiles bringing healing, as he had previously brought healing to the Jews. Now, after preaching to them, he gives them bread, as previously he had given bread to the chosen people. Mark has some signature words to indicate that the context of the first feeding (6:30–44) was Jewish, while the context here is Gentile. In the previous feeding, there were twelve baskets left over; this time there are seven. *Twelve* was the number of tribes among the Jews. *Seven* was the number of pagan nations in Canaan (Palestine) before the Jewish invasion, and seven had become a symbolic number for the Gentile world. The baskets, Greek *kophinoi*, in the first feeding were a particular type of Jewish basket; in the second, *spyrida* is the common term for baskets. In the first Jesus spoke a Jewish blessing, *eulogeō*; in the second, he speaks a Greek blessing, *eucharisteō*, over the bread; and to say that the bread is for both Jew and Gentile, he speaks the Jewish blessing over the fish. He who is God's bread for his chosen people, is bread for all the world's peoples.

Scholars generally believe that there were not two separate feeding instances but two tellings of the one feeding. Such a repetition is termed a "doublet." There are a number of doublets in Matthew, but this is the only one I know of in Mark. In this particular instance, a careful study of grammar and vocabulary has indicated that the narrative Mark inherited from the tradition was the second feeding, not the first. Using this second one as his model, Mark has carefully sculpted the all-important feeding in chapter 6.

BLINDNESS (8:11–21)

The Pharisees Are Blind

[11]The Pharisees came and began to argue with him, asking him for **a sign from heaven**, to test him. [12]And he sighed deeply in his spirit and said, "Why does this generation ask for a sign? Truly I tell you, **no sign** will be given to this generation." [In the Greek Jesus gives a strong triple emphasis to His refusal. The English cannot convey the force of the Greek.] [13]And he left them, and getting into the boat again, he went across to the other side.

At the end of Galilee III, Mark shows a blindness we have come to expect, the blindness of the Pharisees. Jesus had crossed back to the western, Jewish, shore of the sea, to be met by this welcoming committee. They ask him for a "sign from heaven." The word "sign" is rare in Mark, occurring only here and in chapter 13, when the disciples ask what sign will there be of the fall of Jerusalem.[7] The power of God, reaching out in compassion, has been seen many times in Jesus, but this is not enough for these Pharisees. They want some sign coming out of the sky. Jesus not only refuses to have anything to do with that sort of request; he turns his back on that kind of Judaism and gets into the boat to cross back to the eastern, pagan shore. The Gospel has more likelihood of a future there. But he has chosen to depend on these fishermen. Twice before (4:35-41; 6:45-52) in the boat, which should be *their* territory, these fishermen have proved failures. They will fail now still more abysmally.

The Disciples Are Blind

[14]Now the disciples had forgotten to bring any (bread) *loaves of bread*; and they had only *one loaf* with them in the boat. [15]And he cautioned them, saying, "Watch out—beware of the yeast of the Pharisees and the yeast of Herod." [16]They said to one another, "It is because we have no (bread) *loaves of bread*." [17]And becoming

aware of it, Jesus said to them, "Why are you talking about having no (bread) *loaves of bread*? Do you still not perceive or understand? **Are your hearts hardened?** [18]**Do you have eyes, and fail to see? Do you have ears, and fail to hear?** And do you not remember? [19]When I broke the five *loaves* for the five thousand, how many baskets full of (broken pieces) *fragments* did you collect?" They said to him, "Twelve." [20]"And the seven for the four thousand, how many baskets full of (broken pieces) *fragments* did you collect?" And they said to him, "Seven." [21]Then he said to them, "**Do you not yet understand?**"

We are not at all surprised to learn that Jesus is having no success with the Pharisees. The depth of his failure with his disciples is dismaying. In the segment of parables in chapter 4, Jesus had said to them, "To you has been given the secret of the kingdom of God, but **for those outside**, everything comes in parables; in order that '**they may indeed look, but not perceive**, and may indeed **listen, but not understand**; so that they may not turn again and be forgiven'" (4:11). Now his own disciples are among those outside.

The dialogue here is difficult. In chapter 3, the Pharisees and Herodians began plotting to destroy Jesus. The Herodians are symbolic of the secular establishment in Galilee; the Pharisees are symbolic of the "strict" Jews. What does their ferment mean? We might guess that it means something like the spirit that moves them. The disciples, quite obtusely, think he is talking about the shortage of bread. This is the first instance of Jesus talking about one thing and the apostles talking about something altogether different. Mark paints in strong colors the disciples' obtuseness here. They appear to think that Jesus is telling them not to buy bread from the Pharisees or Herodians. Or perhaps they think he is upbraiding them for not bringing enough food. Jesus does more than upbraid them. He becomes absolutely exasperated with them—but not because he has had to miss out on lunch.

Jesus does not pursue the point about the yeast. Instead he takes up their talk about no bread. Notice that they have one loaf with them. This would be barely enough to feed one person, let alone the whole group. Jesus endeavors to take the conversation to a deeper level than mere bread to eat. So he asks them if they cannot see what it all means. He makes use of the two feeding episodes in an endeavor to get them to see. They know what happened each time. They have the right answers. But they cannot see deeper than the miracle itself. We have struck this earlier, at the end of the exodus events in chapter 6, when Mark expressed their blindness: "They were utterly astounded, for **they did not understand about the loaves,** but **their hearts were hardened**" (6:51–52). Here, at the end of Galilee III, their hearts are still hardened. They still do not understand.

But now we have to ask, Understand what? What is the deeper reality they have not seen? For Mark's audience in Rome the meaning may be that Jesus is God's one bread for both Jew (twelve baskets) and Gentile (seven baskets), and that squabbles about food are silly. This answer has been proposed, and it is part of Mark's story under the story. *Within* the story, however—what the apostles are meant to see but do not see—this answer will not do. If the apostles are meant to deduce that Jesus is the one bread for both Jew and Gentile, or else be ranked as outsiders, then the Good News is an impossible cipher. What they are supposed to see but do not see is much more obvious. They still cannot see who Jesus is.

The Pharisees are blind; Jesus' disciples are blind. Jesus has not succeeded with the Pharisees. He has not succeeded with his disciples. At this point, a roll call of those who have accepted the reign of God, which Jesus had set out to establish, would not take very long.

THE CENTER OF THE GOSPEL (8:22–33)

Jesus Cures a Blind Man, but It Is Difficult

22They came to Bethsaida. Some people brought a blind man to him and begged him to touch him. 23He took the blind man by the hand and led him out of the village; and **when he had put saliva**

on his eyes and laid his hands on him, he asked him, "Can you see anything?" [24]And the man looked up and said, "**I can see people, but they look like trees, walking.**" [25]Then Jesus laid his hands on his eyes again; and he looked intently and his sight was restored, and he saw everything clearly. [26]Then he sent him away to his home, saying, "Do not even go into the village."

Mark places this episode from Jesus' life at this strategic point in the story so that the episode can act as a parable. The disciples are blind. Jesus here cures a blind man, but he has difficulty in effecting the cure. Placed at this point in the story, the curing is a pledge that Jesus *will* bring the disciples to see; but it is not going to be easy. Notice that Jesus again uses spittle, an unclean substance. He has crossed the lake; so, as previously, the man is a pagan. To effect a cure Jesus employs at first a means of curing blindness used generally by healers at that time. There is a record of Vespasian curing blindness by that method. Jesus' endeavor is not wholly successful. So he simply places his hands on the man's eyes. Possibly Mark is making a distinction here between using human means, and simply placing it in God's hands.

This episode is reported only in Mark. Once again, the other evangelists were embarrassed by Jesus' possessing the limitations that are part of being human.

Peter Sees

[27]Jesus went on with his disciples to the villages of Caesarea Philippi; and **on the way** he asked his disciples, "Who do **people** say that I am?" [28]And they answered him, "John the Baptist; and others, Elijah; and still others, one of the prophets." [29]He asked them, "But who do you say that I am?" Peter answered him, "You are **the Messiah.**" [30]And he sternly ordered them not to tell anyone about him.

The way people are thinking has already been stated (6:14–16). In this context, "people" are opposed to the disciples.

Consequently, it implies some deficiency. This deficiency will become clear shortly. Peter answers, "You are the Christ." He is the first human being in the story to advance to this understanding. Jesus, for his part, neither denies nor yet affirms with any enthusiasm Peter's answer. He enjoins Peter to silence.

Peter Does Not See

[31] Then he began to teach them that the Son of Man must undergo great suffering, and be rejected by the elders, the chief priests, and the scribes, and be killed, and after three days rise again. [32] He said all this quite openly. And Peter took him aside and began to rebuke him. [33] But turning and looking at his disciples, he rebuked Peter and said, "Get behind me, Satan! For you are setting your mind not on divine things but on human things."

As explained in chapter 2, the linchpin belongs to both halves of the Gospel, completing the first and beginning the second. Mark 8:31–33 will be studied in the next chapter.

Notes

1. The Pharisees' enemies nicknamed them "Persians," and that nickname may have contributed to Mark's twice linking the Pharisees and the Herodians in their plotting against Jesus.

2. I am indebted to Francis J. Moloney, S.D.B., for pointing this out. Some deny that Mark deliberately chooses the verb *teach* here. The evidence of the Gospel is against them. There are thirty-five occurrences of "teach" or a variant such as the noun "teacher" in Mark. In Mark 7, Jesus attacks the Pharisees for *teaching* human customs as doctrines (literally, "teachings"). Apart from that instance, and this present verse, in every reference to teaching in Mark Jesus is the subject. Jesus is called Teacher twelve times. In the final instance of this term (14:4) Jesus refers to himself as "the teacher." Mark is being quite deliberate here. The apostles were sent out to *preach*. On the way they have graduated themselves, and returned as *teachers*.

Words to do with preaching occur twelve times in Mark. Preaching can be about repentance, or the Good News, or the saving acts of Jesus. Preachers include John the Baptist, Jesus, the disciples, various persons whom Jesus has cured. In two instances (1:45; 7:36), these latter preach Jesus after he has explicitly forbidden them to.

3. Following are a few of many Old Testament passages addressing God as Lord of the Sea. The first one also speaks of God passing by, and may have been in Mark's mind when he wrote 6:48. Jb 9:8–11: "God, God alone stretched out the heavens and He treads upon the waves of the sea; God made the Bear and Orion, the Pleiades and the stars of the south; God's works are great, beyond understanding, He does marvelous things beyond reckoning. Look, if He passes by me, I do not see Him; He moves past me, and I do not recognize Him." Jb 38:16: "Have you gone down and discovered the springs of the sea, or seen the sea's dark foundations?" Ps 77:19: "Your way was through the sea, Your path, through the sea's darkest depths; Your footprints went unseen." Is 43:16: "Thus says the LORD, Who made a way in the sea, a path through the depths of the sea." See also Sir 24:5.

4. I am grateful to Jerome Neyrey, who, in a lecture given in Ballarat, Australia, pointed out that, in the Old Testament, God often spoke these words. If Mark did not intend to present Jesus here as actually uttering the divine name, he certainly does intend to convey that Jesus is speaking to his apostles in the way God had often spoken to his people. Because Mark 6:33–52 implies in so many different ways that Jesus is divine, I think that he does present Jesus using the divine name. Later in Mark there are two further possible uses by Jesus of the divine name.

5. Each time Jesus was on the eastern side of the lake of Galilee, he was in predominantly Gentile territory. On the western side, he was in predominantly Jewish territory. All of Galilee had a mixed Jew-Gentile population. In the region of Tyre and Sidon, he was in clearly Gentile territory.

Jesus did not spend a lot of his ministry among Gentiles, nor did he discuss with his disciples the place of Gentiles in their future mission or their relationship with the law of Moses. If he had done so, that would not have been a burning issue for the early church.

6. Ched Myers, *Binding the Strong Man: A Political Reading of Mark's Story of Jesus* (Maryknoll, N.Y.: Orbis Books, 1988), 75.

7. The word occurs twice in Mark 16:9–20, but this is the appendix, which was not written by Mark.

CHAPTER 6

MARK 8:22–10:52

THE JOURNEY TO JERUSALEM

The First Prophecy of the Passion
(8:31–9:29)

We have seen that the linchpin completes the first half of the Gospel. In the linchpin, a human being comes to acknowledge that Jesus is the Christ, the first of the two titles by which the Gospel's heading designates Jesus. It also introduces the second half, in which Jesus endeavors to teach his disciples what the title "the Christ" means, and what following the Christ means. The linchpin begins with the curing of a blind man, a curing that Jesus finds difficult. Mark placed this curing strategically, at the end of Galilee III, after the apostles' blindness has become obvious.

Jesus' teaching discipleship, which is about to commence, is placed in the context of the journey to Jerusalem. The journey was already indicated as a paradigm for discipleship at the beginning of Jesus' ministry with his calling "follow me" (1:18). The journey to Jerusalem is initially signaled within the linchpin at 8:27, "On the way." Caesarea Philippi was in the far north of Galilee. The journey's destination will not become clear until much later. The cure of the blind man, placed right after the episode of the apostles' obtuseness, will find a companion story when Jesus heals another blind man. This healing will occur just as the journey to Jerusalem is ending. The two cures of the blind act as a frame for the journey narrative, thus making that narrative a giant inclusion.

Beginning Frame or Inclusion:
Jesus Cures a Blind Man

8:22They came to Bethsaida. Some people brought a blind man to him and begged him to touch him. 23He took the blind man by the hand and led him out of the village; and when he had put saliva on his eyes and laid his hands on him, he asked him, "Can you see anything?" 24And the man looked up and said, "I can see people, but they look like trees, walking." 25Then Jesus laid his hands on his eyes again; and he looked intently and his sight was restored, and he saw everything clearly. 26Then he sent him away to his home, saying, "Do not even go into the village."

Peter Sees

27Jesus went on with his disciples to the villages of Caesarea Philippi; and **on the way** he asked his disciples, "Who do **people** say that I am?" 28And they answered him, "John the Baptist; and others, Elijah; and still others, one of the prophets." 29He asked them, "But who do you say that I am?" Peter answered him, "You are **the Messiah**." 30And he sternly ordered them not to tell anyone about him.

The Destiny of the Messiah:
Peter's Vision Is Out of Focus

31Then he began to teach them that **the Son of Man** must undergo great suffering, and be rejected by the elders, the chief priests, and the scribes, and be killed, and after three days rise again. 32**He said all this quite openly.** And Peter took him aside and began to (rebuke) *muzzle* him. 33But turning and looking at his disciples, he (rebuked) *muzzled* Peter and said, "**Get (behind me)** *back into my following,* **Satan!** For you are **setting your mind** not on divine things but on **human** things."

Since being a disciple means following Jesus, the place of the disciple is not in front of Jesus or beside him, but behind him. The

Greek word *opisō* expresses this; and indeed when Jesus first called disciples we are told that they followed after *(opisō)* Jesus (1:20). The NRSV's "Get *behind* me," while it expresses Jesus' rebuke, does not capture this fine nuance.

Jesus had made a distinction between the way "people" think and the way the apostles should think, "Who do *people* say that I am . . . but who do *you* say that I am . . . ?" Shortly afterwards, he rebukes Peter, "You do not think *God's* way but *people's* way." By implication then, when Peter said "You are the Christ," since he was not thinking *people's* way, he was thinking *God's* way. Jesus thus obliquely confirms the title Peter has given him; however, he is dismissive of the title. God has led Peter to call Jesus the Christ; but Jesus wants nobody to know that he is the Christ. It is the messianic secret. Because people are bound to misconstrue it, and Peter immediately afterwards does misconstrue it, it is better for them to remain ignorant.

Peter, in calling Jesus the Christ, seemed to see clearly. His rejecting the destiny that Jesus announces for himself reveals that Peter's vision is quite blurred. Peter tries to muzzle Jesus; Jesus does muzzle Peter. Peter has called Jesus the Christ; Jesus calls Peter Satan. For a moment Peter was thinking as God thinks; now he is thinking not in God's way but in the way people without faith would think. Peter's heart is set on what the world calls victory. Jesus commands Peter to get back behind him, where a follower should be.[1]

The Son of Man

Rather than be called Messiah, Jesus adopts for himself another title—Son of Man. This term has appeared twice already, in chapter 2; but there it was possibly the author speaking, not Jesus. In that chapter it was referring to Jesus as one with great authority, authority such that he is able to forgive sins, authority such that he is master even of the Sabbath. That kind of sovereign authority evokes an extremely important Son-of-Man passage in the book of Daniel. Daniel is one of the last written books of the Hebrew Bible. In 167 B.C.E. the ruler of Syria, to whom Judea was vassal at that time, launched a savage persecution of the Jews. The Jews had suffered many wars, conflicts, and invasions during their history, but this was the first time that they had ever been made to suffer precisely for their faithfulness to God's covenant. Led by Judas Maccabeus (a nickname that means "the hammer"), who belonged to one of the priestly families, some of the Jews revolted. Daniel was written during the ensuing persecution and civil war to encourage the Jews to keep faith with God. Incidentally, against all odds, the revolt was eventually successful. The writer of Daniel employed various images, visions, and stories of past heroes to encourage fidelity. In chapter 7 he paints a picture of a victorious Son of Man. As it stands in the book of Daniel, Son of Man is a code name for all the faithful, persecuted Jews; and they are promised final victory. The author of course was putting his life at risk by writing the book and so needed to write in code, describing visions and the like that would have been indecipherable to the persecutors. When victory did come, when the persecution had ceased, and when its memory had faded, the Son-of-Man prophecy began to be seen as not yet ultimately fulfilled. Hopes were attached to a coming Son of Man. Because of the sufferings of this Son of Man, he is linked in Mark's Gospel (and, as far as is known, never by any previous writer) to the faithful Suffering Servant of God about whom Isaiah had spoken in four separate oracles. (The Servant Song passages are Is 42:1–7; 49:1–6; 50:4–9; and 52:13–53:12. A fifth passage, Is 61:1–9 came to be ranked with the Servant Songs). In Dn 7:9–14, the beasts who are crushed are symbols of all the powers that have oppressed God's people:

> As I watched, thrones were set in place, and the Ancient of Days took His throne, His clothing was as white as the snow, and the hair of His head was like pure white wool; His throne was like flames of fire, and its wheels were like burning fire. [10]A stream of fire flowed out from His seat. A thousand thousands were ministering to Him, and ten thousand times ten thousand stood and waited upon Him. A court was convened and the books were opened. [11]I watched . . . and as I watched, the beast was slain, and its body destroyed and consumed in the fire. [12]As for the rest of the beasts, their power was broken, but their lives were prolonged for a time and a season. [13]As

I gazed into the visions of the night I saw one like a Son of Man coming upon the clouds of heaven. And he came to the Ancient of Days and was presented before Him. [14]On him was conferred dominion and glory and kingship, so that all peoples and nations, and languages should serve him. His kingdom is an everlasting kingdom that shall not pass away, and his kingship is one that shall never be destroyed.

The first time Jesus designates himself as Son of Man is in this passage (8:31), but he is talking not primarily about being victorious but about suffering, being rejected and put to death. Jesus prefers to designate himself as Son of Man because Son of Man could be simply an indirect third-person way of referring to oneself. If I wrote "the present author believes . . . ," I would be referring to myself, but in the third person. Son of Man was often used in this way, and we can find it so used many times in the book of Ezechiel. It's a much safer self-designation for Jesus to use than Messiah; there was much less danger of being misunderstood.

Later in the Gospel (10:45) Jesus will speak of himself both as Son of Man and as Suffering Servant: "the Son of Man came not to be served but to serve, and to *give His life as a ransom for many."* The italicized phrase comes directly from the fourth of the Servant Songs.

At 8:31 then, Jesus begins to teach his disciples what his destiny—the destiny of the Christ—will be. Three times in the course of the journey Jesus will tell them that he is going to be rejected and put to death. He has bound the disciples to silence about his being the Messiah. He binds no one to silence about his destiny. He speaks quite openly, for everyone to hear.

Discipleship

[34]He called the crowd with his disciples, and said to them, "If any want to become my followers, let them deny themselves and take up their cross and follow me. [35]For those who want to save their life will lose it, and those who lose their life **for my sake, and for the sake of the gospel,** will save it. [36]For what will it profit them to gain the whole world and forfeit their life? [37]Indeed, what can they give in return for their life? [38]Those who are ashamed **of me**

and of my words in this adulterous and sinful generation, of them the Son of Man will also be ashamed when he comes in the glory of his Father with the holy angels." [9:1]And he said to them, "Truly I tell you, there are some standing here who will not taste death until they see that the kingdom of God has come with power."

This passage is difficult. Mark is employing a preaching and writing technique of the time called "stringing beads." In this technique the speaker or writer moves from one thought to another by means of link- or "hook"-words; or sometimes the link is by one thought giving rise naturally to the next. In such discourse, the final thought may be far removed from the first thought. Jesus is outrageous here. He is making himself absolute. No reasonable person would dare to make the demands that he makes of his followers. The follower must deny himself and take up his cross . . . anyone who loses his life for my sake . . . will save it. Jesus is demanding for himself a loyalty owed only to God.

The journey to Jerusalem is a journey to Jesus' passion. On the way he tries three times to prepare his disciples for the coming disaster, and each time he tries to help them understand what it means to be following behind the Son of Man. He tells them that he is going to be put to death; he tells not only them but also "the crowd" (who by definition cannot understand [cf. 8:27, 33]) that his followers must first take up the cross, and *only then* follow. Is he speaking with Semitic hyperbole, exaggeration? He is and he is not. He himself, for his faithfulness to the gospel, will have to take up the cross; and some of his followers in Rome have suffered crucifixion for his sake.

If Semites talk beautifully in hyperbole, they also talk beautifully in parallels. "For my sake, and for the sake of the gospel" is paralleled by "of me and of my words." Since the latter refers to Jesus' words about his passion and our following, that is also what "gospel" means here. "Those who want to save their life will lose it" is a foil for its parallel "those who lose their life for my sake, and for the sake of the gospel, will save it." It is not difficult to hear Jesus speaking directly to the Christian community in Rome. But his immediate audience, disciples and crowd, is left wondering. "Those who want to save their life will lose it" is a parable, a riddle. We seem to know what it means. If we are asked to explain it we may perhaps attempt to give examples of what it means. Giving examples is one thing; defining it is another. We will say that Jesus is talking about life on two different levels. Asked what those levels are, we find that we are afraid to tie it down, to be exact.

"For what will it profit anyone to gain the whole world and forfeit their life? Indeed, what can they give in return for their life?" Once again, Jesus seems here to be speaking of those who, in the persecution, had failed. But in the Gospel narrative itself Jesus is warning his own disciples. The test, the moment of decision, will come soon for them. Yet this saying seemingly contradicts the earlier "Those who want to save their life will lose it." The *world* that is not worth trading in exchange for your life is evidently the same as the *life*, the saving of which means we lose life.

"Those who are ashamed of me and of my words in this adulterous and sinful generation, of them the Son of Man will also be ashamed when he comes in the glory of his Father with the holy angels." The word shame appears here, the opposite of honor. Jesus speaks of people who may be ashamed of him and his words . . . What words? The words he has just spoken about his destiny, and the need to follow him. When the time comes, not only the crowds but his own disciples *will be* ashamed. What will Jesus do to them? The code of honor and shame demands that he bring shame on them. When the time comes, he will not do what he threatens. The young man in white will simply say, "Go and tell his disciples and Peter . . ." (16:7).

Jesus speaks of an "adulterous and sinful generation." Whom does he mean? A short time before (8:12) he had condemned the generation that demands a sign. Is it that generation, the Pharisees who demanded a sign, that Jesus now calls adulterous and sinful? When it comes to his capture and trial, they are not even present.

His words are more puzzling still, "the Son of Man will also be ashamed when he comes in the glory of his Father with the holy angels." He speaks of the Son of Man coming in the glory of his Father. Mark certainly intends to evoke Daniel 7. There God is surrounded by millions of angels, and there the Son of Man has glory conferred on him. When is that to be? Is it the parousia, the last judgment? It seems so to us, and it would have seemed so to Mark's original hearers in Rome. Mark will tell us soon that Jesus will be in his glory (which comes from his Father) when he is hanging on a cross.

"And he said to them, 'Truly I tell you, there are some standing here who will not taste death until they see that the kingdom of God has come with power.'"[2] This verse certainly looks immediately ahead to the Transfiguration ("see" will be repeated immediately after the Transfiguration, so it is a frame). However, it would seem to be talking about the parousia, the time when Christ will come again, for the preceding verse seems to be talking about the parousia. In Daniel 7, the Son of Man has conferred on him not only glory but power and sovereignty, eternal kingship. If Jesus' coming in glory means the cross, then his coming in power means the cross too. So the reign of God coming in power is about the cross. What strange glory! What strange power? Mark's account of the passion is replete with images of kingship.

The Transfiguration

9:1And he said to them, "Truly I tell you, there are some standing here who will not taste death until they **see** that the kingdom of God has come with power."

2**Six days later,** Jesus took with him Peter and James and John, and led them up a high mountain apart, by themselves. And he was transfigured before them, 3and his clothes became dazzling white, such as no one on earth could bleach them. 4And there appeared to them **Elijah** with **Moses,** who were talking with Jesus. 5Then Peter said to Jesus, "Rabbi, it is good for us to be here; let us make **three dwellings, one for you, one for Moses, and one for Elijah."** 6He did not know what to say, for they were terrified. 7Then a cloud overshadowed them, and from the cloud there came a voice, "**This is my Son, the Beloved; listen to him!**" 8Suddenly when they looked around, they saw no one with them any more, but only Jesus. 9As they were coming down the mountain, he ordered them to tell no one about what **they had seen**, until after the Son of Man had risen from the dead. ¹⁰So they kept the matter to themselves, questioning what this rising from the dead could mean.

Jesus had refused a sign to a generation that asked for one (8:12). He has described that generation as adulterous and sinful (8:38). To Peter, James, and John, a sign is now given. The disciples do not belong to the generation Jesus condemns.

The second and decisive title of Jesus, "the Son of God" suddenly appears here. The three disciples are told by God who Jesus is. Peter's suggestion that they build three tents would place Jesus on an equal footing with Moses and Elijah. The voice that speaks from the cloud places him far above them. The words God adds, "Listen to him," are an assurance to the disciples that this Jesus, who makes outrageous demands, knows what he is talking about. As his disciples, learning from him, they are on the right path. As the story develops from here, it becomes apparent that this sign from heaven makes no difference. The disciples will try to teach the teacher. In the moment of testing, they will become deserters. And for Jesus himself—the sign from heaven will not prevent him from crying out at the end, "My God, my God, why have You deserted me?"

Mark emphasizes the presence of Moses and Elijah. They are mentioned five times in the seven verses. Moses and Elijah together epitomized the covenant: Moses the Law, Elijah the Prophets. Each of them met with God on Mount Sinai. By commencing "six days later," Mark evokes those earlier theophanies (revelations of God) at Mount Sinai. Very rarely does Mark specify time. If he does so here, it is for a reason: Moses met with God on the mountain on the seventh day (Ex 24:16): "The glory of the LORD settled on the mountain of Sinai, and the cloud covered it for six days; on the seventh day the LORD called to Moses from out of the cloud." Six days later means on the seventh day.

Though Peter is the speaker, all three disciples are implicated in getting Jesus wrong here. Peter did not know what to say, because *they* were exceedingly afraid. This failure of the disciples to grasp what Jesus has said is emphasized at the end, "They kept the matter to themselves, questioning what rising from the dead could mean." Mark paints with heavy colors the obtuseness of the disciples. Herod had thought that Jesus was John the Baptist risen from the dead. The disciples do not know what rising from the dead means. It is not surprising that the three cannot grasp the *suffering* Messiah; they cannot grasp even *resurrection.*

Elijah—John the Baptist

11Then they asked him, "Why do the scribes say that Elijah must come first?" 12He said to them, "Elijah is indeed coming first to restore all things. How then is it written about the Son of Man, that he is to go through many sufferings and be treated with contempt? 13But I tell you that Elijah has come, and they did to him whatever they pleased, as it is written about him."

The last book of the Hebrew Bible is the prophet Malachi. The final verses of that prophet read as follows: "Behold, I will send you **the prophet Elijah** before the day of the LORD comes, the great and terrible day. He will turn the hearts of fathers to their children and the hearts of children to their fathers, lest I come and strike the land with a curse" (4:5–6). The presence of Elijah in the Transfiguration prompts the three disciples to ask about this coming of Elijah. There was no expectation that Elijah (who had not died but was taken up into heaven in a fiery chariot) would prepare the way for the Messiah. He would prepare for the Day of the Lord. The disciples are confused. At the beginning of the Gospel, Mark had identified John the Baptist as that Elijah who was to come. Now the same identification is found on Jesus' lips. The disciples, considering John the Baptist's fate, do not see how he could be that Elijah. Jesus does not directly answer their difficulty but points to his own destiny, the destiny of the Son of Man: "he is to go through many sufferings and be treated with contempt." The fate of the Elijah they were expecting is of a piece with what is going to be Jesus' fate.

A Final Exorcism

[14]When they came to the disciples, they saw a great crowd around them, and some scribes arguing with them. [15]When the whole crowd saw him, they were immediately overcome with awe, and they ran forward to greet him. [16]He asked them, "What are you arguing about with them?" [17]Someone from the crowd answered him, "Teacher, I brought you my son; he has a spirit that makes him unable to speak; [18]and whenever it seizes him, it dashes him down; and he foams and grinds his teeth and becomes rigid; and I asked your disciples to cast it out, but they could not do so." [19]He answered them, **"You faithless generation**, how much longer must I be among you?[3] How much longer must I put up with you? Bring him to me." [20]And they brought the boy to him. When the spirit saw him, immediately it convulsed the boy, and he fell on the ground and rolled about, foaming at the mouth. [21]Jesus asked the father, "How long has this been happening to him?" And he said, "From childhood. [22]It has often cast him into the fire and into the water, to destroy him; but if you are able to do anything, have pity on us and help us." [23]Jesus said to him, "If you are able!—All things can be done for the one who believes." [24]Immediately the father of the child cried out, **"I believe; help my unbelief!"** [25]When Jesus saw that a crowd came running together, he rebuked the unclean spirit, saying to it, "You spirit that keeps this boy from speaking and hearing, I command you, come out of him, and never enter him again!" [26]After crying out and convulsing him terribly, it came out, and the boy was like a corpse, so that most of them said, "He is dead." [27]But Jesus took him by the hand and lifted him up, and he was able to stand. [28]When he had entered the house, his disciples asked him privately, **"Why could we not cast it out?"** [29]He said to them, **"This kind can come out only through prayer."**

Fresh from the moment of revelation Jesus is confronted with the mess of life. Some details of this episode are quite puzzling. Mark *seems* to have taken over a story from the tradition; and he *seems* not to have succeeded in reshaping it quite to his purpose. Why, when the crowd sees him, are they immediately overcome?

Only the father speaks, but Jesus answers *them*. Jesus has called
some Pharisees "a generation that demands a sign." He has spoken of "this adulterous and sinful generation." Now he speaks in
exasperated tones to the "faithless generation," and this is
directed primarily to his own disciples. A contrast is made
between the simple dependent cry of the boy's father and the
unsuccessful self-reliance of the apostles. The answer Jesus gives
when they ask why they were not successful drips with irony,
"This kind can be driven out only through prayer." How without
prayer can a disciple drive out any demon? Jesus, though he has
barely returned from the Mount of the Transfiguration, has not
himself prayed over the boy to drive out the demon. Nor has Mark
stated that Jesus ascended the mountain to pray. The praying
upon which Jesus insists is rather the utter reliance on God. The
cry of the boy's father is such a prayer of surrender.

The Second Prophecy of the Passion
(9:30–10:31)

Second Prophecy of the Passion

³⁰They went on from there and passed through Galilee. **He did not
want anyone to know** it; ³¹for **he was teaching his disciples,** saying to them, "The Son of Man is to be betrayed into human hands,
and they will kill him, and three days after being killed, he will rise
again." ³²But **they did not understand what he was saying and
were afraid to ask him.**

Mark emphasizes here that Jesus is teaching his disciples. He
has tried with the leaders, and with the crowd, and he has failed.
He needs to prepare some, the few, to keep the Gospel alive when
he is gone. The impression given here is that he wants to keep
secret his coming fate. Yet, when he spoke about it first (8:31–32),
he did so "quite openly." His judgment now is that there is no
point in telling the crowd even bad news. However, the reaction
of his own disciples is "we do not understand," and "we do not
want to understand."

As previously, Jesus does not specify *how* he will meet his death. As previously, too, he states that on the third day he will rise again. We cannot answer with certainty whether this confidence that he would rise from the dead on the third day lay within the realm of special knowledge, given to him by his Father or is simply an expression of his trust in his Father that death will not be the end. In my seminary days it was presumed that Jesus knew everything, but that really diminishes his sharing our humanness. There is no reason to reject the second opinion, that the "pioneer of our Faith" had to live in faith himself. Indeed, if he saw clearly the resurrection that lay ahead of him, how could there be an Agony in the Garden, or that cry from the cross? In Old Testament writings, the third day is often the day when God steps in to have his say.[4] Parts of the Old Testament—the Servant Songs in Isaiah, Psalm 22, the book of Wisdom—gave Jesus good reason to trust that he would be vindicated.

Discipleship

[33]Then they came to Capernaum; and when he was in the house he asked them, "What were you arguing about on the way?" [34]But **they were silent,** for on the way they had argued with one another **who was the greatest.** [35]He sat down, called the Twelve, and said to them, "Whoever *(hōs)* wants to be first must be last of all and servant of all." [36]Then he took a little child and put it among them; and taking it in his arms, he said to them, [37]"Whoever *(hōs)* welcomes one such child in my name *(onomati)* welcomes me, and whoever *(hōs)* welcomes me welcomes not me but the one who sent me."

At the beginning of Jesus' ministry, the quality of the disciples' enthusiasm (1:37: "everybody is looking for you") suggested that their agenda might be different from Jesus' agenda. That is confirmed now. Jesus is trying to prepare them for his coming passion, and they are arguing about who among them is the greatest—as though, apart from Jesus, the memory of any of them would have long survived their death. They have greatness all wrong. Their silence when Jesus questions them is an admission that their thinking is wrong. Jesus tries to teach them what real greatness, the greatness of the kingdom is about: serving even the least. Some people may find vv. 36–37 jarring. The jarring is a reaction to our religious upbringing. We were told that we had to love people for Jesus' sake, or to love Jesus in them. This is condescension rather than love. Any kind of love that says "You are really not lovable; but for Jesus' sake I will love you (and aren't I wonderful for doing that)" is a caricature of love. In fact, we would expect Jesus to say at this point what he does not say until 10:14: "It is to such as these (the little children) that the kingdom of God belongs. Truly I tell you, whoever does not receive the kingdom of God as a little child will never enter it." Mark does not develop the present incident further because, when we come to that later episode (10:13–16), he wants us to notice that the disciples have not listened to what Jesus is teaching them now. Jesus identifies himself with the least, with the little children. When next Jesus tries to prepare them for his passion (10:32–34), they will still be jockeying for places; and he will identify himself as a servant.

Three of the Twelve, Peter, James and John, were the privileged witnesses of the Theophany on the mountain. While Mark points out the failure of all the disciples, he highlights the failure of these three. John is wrong here on two counts. The first is a possessiveness about the reign of God that would make it their fiefdom rather than God's reign. The other is their making themselves equal with Jesus. In chapter 6, we saw the Twelve graduating from discipleship, declaring themselves to be teachers. Here John rejects one who is not in the following of *us*. They are making themselves the equals of Jesus.

Possessive Discipleship

[38]**John** said to him, "Teacher, we saw someone casting out demons in your name *(onomati)*, and we tried to stop him, because **he was not following us**." [39]But Jesus said, "Do not stop him; for no one who does a deed of power in my name *(onomati)* will be able soon afterward to speak evil of me. [40]Whoever *(hōs)* is not against us is for us.

In the course of his narrative, Mark gives several examples of outsiders who are really insiders. Mark's persistence with this theme suggests that his community in Rome, despite its failure in the persecution, continues to view itself as superior to the world outside of it that has no knowledge of Jesus. This present instance of an outsider who is really an insider is, in the story thus far, Mark's strongest enunciation of this theme; and it stands as an enduring warning to us. To the extent that the church gathers disciples *for itself rather than for Christ* it has ceased to follow him.

[41]"For truly I tell you, whoever *(hōs)* gives you a cup of water to drink because you bear the name *(onomati)* of Christ will by no means lose the reward. [42]If any of you *(hōs)* put a stumbling block *(skandalisē)* before one of these little ones who believe in me, it would be better for you if a great millstone were hung around your neck and you were thrown into the sea. [43]If your hand causes you to stumble *(skandalizē)*, cut it off; it is better for you to enter life *(zōēn)* maimed than to have two hands and to go to hell *(geennan)*, to the unquenchable fire. [45]And if your foot causes you to stumble *(skandalizē)*, cut it off; it is better for you to enter life *(zōēn)* lame than to have two feet and to be thrown into hell *(geennan)*. [47]And if your eye causes you to stumble *(skandalizē)*, tear it out; it is better for you to enter the kingdom of God with one eye than to have two eyes and to be thrown into hell *(geennan)*, [48]where their worm never dies, and the fire *(pyr)* is never quenched. [49]For everyone will be salted *(halisthēsetai)* with fire *(pyri)*. [50]Salt *(halas)* is good; but if salt *(halas)* has lost its saltiness *(analon)*, how can you season it? Have salt *(hala)* in yourselves, and be at peace with one another."

As previously (8:34–9:1), the stringing of beads technique has been used to join some disparate teachings of Jesus. The stringing is made by hook-words that are not as obvious in translation as they are in the original Greek. The bead-stringing begins with v. 36. I have treated the unit vv. 38–40 separately; but the bead-stringing indicates that it belongs to this segment. In fact, Jesus' mention of "little ones" links this passage back to the teaching about true greatness. I have inserted into the text a transliteration of the hook-words that make a unity of the segment. To properly sense the continuity artificially created by these hook words one would, of course, need to read and understand the Greek text. The reader will probably notice that v. 44 and v. 46 are missing. They were inserted into the text of Mark by some copyist. Having been recognized by the text critics as certainly interpolations, they are omitted. When such excisions are made the remaining verses are never renumbered. That would cause confusion (between old and new versions). The saying in v. 41 flows on from v. 40. It would be pure guesswork to say what situation in Mark's community in Rome is being addressed. Verse 42 addresses sophisticated Christians who are needlessly upsetting those in the community less capable—the little ones.

Verses 43, 45, and 47 are parallel to one another. The same point is made by examples drawn from different members of the body. The examples employ Semitic hyperbole. Not even the most rabid fundamentalist feels compelled to take Jesus literally; and neither hand, nor foot, nor eye enjoys a life of its own. The reign of God spoken of in v. 47 is not God's rule in our lives here; rather it is heaven itself. In the parallel instances (vv. 43, 45) Jesus calls it not the kingdom but *life*.

In Greek, the word translated as "hell" is the equivalent of Gehenna. This is not a Greek but an Aramaic word transliterated into Greek. Mark does not translate Gehenna. Presumably the word, like *Hosanna, Alleluia,* and *Amen* had passed into Christian usage without translation. This is, incidentally the only mention of hell in the Gospel of Mark. The description given of hell, "where their worm never dies, and the fire is never quenched" is drawn from the prophet Isaiah: "As they shall go out they shall see the corpses of the people who have rebelled against me; for their worm shall not die, their fire shall not be put out, and they shall be a thing of horror to all flesh" (66:24).[5]

In several places in this segment there may be reference to cult (salt was used in some sacrifices). Consequently, it is *possible* that vv. 43–47 may be a reversal of values. In the Temple only animals or firstfruits without blemish could be offered. Similarly, priests with some blemish could not perform the rituals of the Temple sacrifice. To be missing a hand or foot or eye was to be blemished and disqualified. There may be here, then, a picture of those who look good going to perdition; while those who are discarded are entering into life. This interpretation would link vv. 43–44 with both the preceding segment and the next large segment, 10:1–31.[6]

Verse 48 is about those in hell; but v. 49, "everyone will be salted with fire," joined to the preceding by the hook-word "fire," refers to the disciples. Fire was used by Christians as a metaphor for persecution. For the Roman Christians death by fire was already stark reality. The meaning of the link-word "salt" in the next phrase—"Salt is good; but if salt has lost its saltiness, how can you season it?"—is not at all clear. "Have salt in yourselves" may mean "be strong in yourselves." Jesus is saying to them, and to Mark's Christians in Rome, "The discipleship of every one of you will be put to the test severely; but be at peace."

The segment made up of vv. 41–50 is even more difficult than the previous one (8:34–9:1), which employed the stringing-of-beads technique. The last two verses (49–50) are notoriously obscure. Those who are just learning this Gospel need not feel deprived if these verses are simply consigned to the too-hard basket. They are not of paramount importance, nor are they the key needed to interpret the whole story. The Roman lectionary in its cycle of Sunday readings has mercifully cut this episode short, omitting these last two verses.

The next section is termed "reversal of values." As mentioned above, Mark may have intended Jesus' ignoring of accepted values in regard to Temple cult to lead into the examples of discipleship he is about to give. Each of these examples turns upside down the values of the disciples' cultural world.

Reversal of Values

Divorce

10:1 He left that place **and went to the region of Judea** and beyond the Jordan. And crowds again gathered around him; and, as was his custom, he again taught them. [2]Some Pharisees came, and to test him they asked, "Is it lawful for a man to divorce his wife?" [3]He answered them, "What did Moses command you?" [4]They said, "Moses allowed a man to write a certificate of dismissal and to divorce her." [5]But Jesus said to them, "Because of your hardness of heart he wrote this commandment for you. [6]But from the beginning of creation, 'God made them male and female.' [7]'For this reason a man shall leave his father and mother and be joined to his wife, [8]and the two shall become one flesh.' So they are no longer two, but one flesh. [9]Therefore what God has joined together, let no one separate." [10]Then in the house the disciples asked him again about this matter. [11]He said to them, "Whoever divorces his wife and marries another commits adultery **against her;** [12]and **if she divorces her husband** and marries another, she commits adultery."

In the patriarchal world of the Jews, if a married man engaged in sexual intercourse with a single woman, he was not guilty of adultery. If he had sex with a married woman, he was guilty of adultery: he had violated her husband's rights. Too much can be made of the following statement, but officially a woman was her husband's property.[7] Moses had allowed a man to divorce his wife. In Jesus' time there was a running dispute among the rabbis about what constituted legitimate grounds for divorce. The followers of the Rabbi Shammai reckoned adultery to be the only just grounds for divorce. The followers of the Rabbi Hillel held that lesser matters such as being a poor cook could justify divorce. This dispute may lie behind the Pharisees' testing of Jesus here. Jesus' answer is radical. First, he teaches that divorce was never in God's intention. Moses allowed divorce because of people's hardheartedness.[8] In saying this, Jesus was making a distinction between the law of Moses and the law of God. Then he says that if a man divorces his wife he commits adultery *against her.* Thus he rules out the shabby chauvinism that would make a woman not the equal of her husband but his chattel. Mark adds, "and *if she divorces her husband* and marries another, she commits adultery." As was pointed out in chapter 1, this made no sense in

Palestine, where women could not divorce their husbands. Mark reinterprets Jesus' teaching for his community in Rome, where women *could* divorce their husbands.

Jews of Jesus' time generally regarded divorce as a great evil. In fact one of the rabbis said that when a man divorces his wife the very altar weeps. This was about as close as the rabbi dared come to saying that God weeps, but the idea of no divorce at all was unthinkable.

Children

¹³People were bringing little children to him in order that he might touch them; and the disciples spoke sternly to them. ¹⁴But when Jesus saw this, he was indignant and said to them, "Let the little children come to me; do not stop them; for it is to such as these that the kingdom of God belongs. ¹⁵Truly I tell you, **whoever does not receive the kingdom of God as a little child will never enter it.**" ¹⁶And he took them up in his arms, laid his hands on them, and blessed them.

The reaction of the disciples here indicates that they have ignored Jesus' earlier words about welcoming children (8:37). Among the Jews, children mattered in the private domain. There they received plenty of affection and attention. In the public domain, they were meant to be seen but not heard; they did not belong in the public domain. Jesus not only welcomes affectionately these children, but holds them up as models for living under God's reign. There are as many interpretations of "receiving the kingdom of God as a little child" as there are interpreters. The quality Jesus referred to is, in my opinion, the ability to receive, to accept, to be dependent, to be powerless.

Wealth

¹⁷As he was setting out **on a journey**, a man ran up and knelt before him, and asked him, "Good Teacher, what must I do to inherit eternal life?" ¹⁸Jesus said to him, "Why do you call me

good? No one is good but God alone. [19]You know the command-ments: 'You shall not murder; You shall not commit adultery; You shall not steal; You shall not bear false witness; You shall not defraud; Honor your father and mother.'" [20]He said to him, "Teacher, **I have kept all these since my youth.**" [21]Jesus, looking at him, loved him and said, "You lack one thing; go, sell what you own, and give the money to the poor, and you will have treasure in heaven; then come, follow me." [22]When he heard this, he was shocked and went away grieving, for he had many possessions.

[23]Then Jesus looked around and said to his disciples, **"How hard it will be for those who have wealth to enter the kingdom of God!"** [24]And the disciples were perplexed at these words. But Jesus said to them again, "Children, how hard it is to enter the kingdom of God! [25]It is easier for a camel to go through the eye of a needle than for someone who is rich to enter the kingdom of God." [26]They were greatly astounded and said to one another, "Then who can be saved?" [27]Jesus looked at them and said, "For mortals it is impossible, but not for God; for God all things are possible."

Explanations bordering on the ingenious have been given of "a camel passing through the eye of a needle." They are quite unnec-essary. Jesus was a Semite. Semites talk beautifully in pictures; and Semites talk in hyperbole. Jesus' purpose was to shock them into taking seriously what he had said.

Fundamentalists have been known to find in Jesus' question "Why do you call me good?" an affirmation of his divinity. At the opposite pole, the lowest of low Christologists rejoice to find here Jesus asserting that he is a sinner. Both explanations are wide of the mark. The man is simply flattering Jesus, a common enough Semitic custom still today. Etiquette demanded that Jesus return flattery with flattery. Jesus avoids returning the flattery; but avoids it gently, by asking the question. I imagine Jesus answering the man's flattery with a wry grin on his face.

The man wants to know what he needs to do to inherit eternal life. In 9:42–50 life and the reign of God were spoken of inter-changeably. The same is true here. The man wants to know what to do to get to heaven. If his answer to Jesus, "Teacher, I have kept all these since my youth" is arrogant or foolhardy, there is no rebuke from Jesus. Instead, Jesus makes an outrageous demand of him, akin to the demand that we take up our cross and follow him. Here Jesus *is* asserting his uniqueness. Following him is more fundamental than are the commandments.

Notice now Jesus' serenity. The man goes away. Jesus does not run after him. He does not say "Wait, you have misunderstood me." He simply lets him go. That man, like all of Jesus' mission, is in the hands of his Father.

Among the Jews, wealth was seen as a sign of God's blessing. When Jesus said, "How hard it will be for those who have wealth to enter the kingdom of God!" he was turning upside down a whole value system. When the disciples register astonishment, Jesus states it more strongly still, and they become even more astonished. Their discouraged cry, "Then who can be saved?" brings words from Jesus to encourage us all.

Mark has given some examples of the way of life Jesus calls us to. They must not be treated as a comprehensive code. We need rather to capture the spirit that inspires them.

The Rewards of Discipleship

28Peter began to say to him, **"Look, we have left everything and followed you."** 29Jesus said, "Truly I tell you, there is no one who has left house or brothers or sisters or mother or father or children or fields, for my sake and for the sake of the good news, 30who will not receive a hundredfold now in this age—houses, brothers and sisters, mothers and children, and fields, **with persecutions**—and in the age to come eternal life. 31But many who are first will be last, and the last will be first.

Just as Jesus took seriously the claim of the rich man that he had always kept the commandments, so now he takes seriously the claim of Peter, "Look, we have left everything and followed you." Jesus' reply to Peter is the sole instance in the whole Gospel of his making earthly promises to those who forsake all to follow him. The addition Mark makes, "with persecutions," sounds out of place, but it is necessary in this Gospel for a community that has known persecution to the death. Verse 31 is a warning against smugness.

In the journey thus far, Jesus has been trying to teach his followers what it means to follow. He has tried to prepare them for his approaching fate. The disciples stumble along, struggling to keep up with him. The next line of the Gospel will mention the destination of the journey for the first time. In addition, Mark deftly paints the picture of Jesus striding ahead, the disciples confused, and Mark's community in Rome afraid. In v. 32 below there are two groups following Jesus. Since the first group is Jesus' disciples, the second group of followers are not people within the story but Mark's community.[9]

Third Prophecy of the Passion
(10:32–52)

Third Prophecy of the Passion

[32]They were **on the road, going up to Jerusalem**, and Jesus was walking ahead of them; they were amazed, **and those who followed were afraid.** He took the Twelve aside again and began to tell them what was to happen to him, [33]saying, "See, we are going up to Jerusalem, and the Son of Man will be handed over to the chief priests and the scribes, and they will condemn him to death; **then they will hand him over to the Gentiles;** [34]they will mock him, and spit upon him, and flog him, and kill him; and after three days he will rise again."

Jesus describes in greater detail what awaits him in Jerusalem. Yet still he does not say that he will be crucified. It hardly took a special revelation to him from his Father for Jesus to discern that his death was being plotted. But did he know it would be by crucifixion? Is that what he means by being handed over to the Gentiles—that the authorities in Jerusalem were determined to inflict on him the supreme degradation? Or did he live with uncertainty about that?

Discipleship

[35]James and John, the sons of Zebedee, came forward to him and said to him, "Teacher, we want you to do for us whatever we ask of you." [36]And he said to them, "What is it you want me to do for you?" [37]And they said to him, **"Grant us to sit, one at your right hand and one at your left, in your glory."** [38]But Jesus said to them, "You do not know what you are asking. Are you able to **drink the cup** that I drink, or **be baptized** with the baptism that I am baptized with?" [39]They replied, **"We are able."** Then Jesus said to them, "The cup that I drink you will drink; and with the baptism with which I am baptized, you will be baptized; [40]**but to sit at my right hand or at my left is not mine to grant, but it is for those for whom it has been prepared."**

There are numerous passages in the Old Testament where "drinking the cup" means suffering. To drain a cup of wine means to take in the bitter dregs at the bottom. Similarly, Baptism originally and properly meant drowning. Both of the images that Jesus uses are images of suffering.

When Jesus made the previous prophecy of his passion, the disciples were arguing about which of them was the greatest. He speaks now a third time, and two of the three who witnessed the theophany seek places of worldly greatness in his worldly empire. The agenda of the pupils is completely contrary to the agenda of the master. Jesus challenges them in words that Mark has arranged very deliberately in order to tell his community what it means to drink Christ's cup in Communion and what it means to accept the sacrament of Baptism. It is accepting suffering. Peter and John confidently assert that they can accept any suffering that being Jesus' followers might entail. This brash assertion marks definitively the failure of the disciples. They are self-made. Their reliance is upon themselves. Not until their proud arrogance crashes will Jesus be able to begin.

They want seats on his right and on his left in his glory. Mark's phrasing (in Greek) deftly places two brigands on his right and on his left in his glory. That happens on the cross. Mark's readers then, recalling these words, will know that the Son of Man's coming in glory is on the cross, and that knowledge calls into question all our assumptions about honor and power. More deeply still, if that is the glory of God, at last fully revealed to us, then it overturns our images of God.

[41]When the ten heard this, **they began to be angry with James and John.** [42]So Jesus called them and said to them, "You know that among the Gentiles those whom they recognize as their rulers lord it over them, and their great ones are tyrants over them. [43]But it is not so among you; but whoever wishes to become great among you must be your **servant,** [44]and whoever wishes to be first among you must be **slave** of all. [45]For the Son of Man came not to be served but to serve, and **to give his life a ransom for many.**"

Slave is, of course, a more extreme word than servant, but too much should not be made of it. The parallel way of speaking required a stronger word to match servant, because first is a more extreme word than great. The ten are angry because James and John were trying to get ahead of them in the race for the best positions. If the other disciples had been angry because the brothers had turned aside from true discipleship, Jesus would have addressed them quite differently.

For the first time, Jesus gives the meaning of his approaching death: he is giving his life to be a ransom for many. In Semitic usage, "many" means all. So Jesus sees his death as having a universal significance. Mark's phrasing draws on the fourth of Isaiah's Servant Songs (52:13–53:12). Isaiah 53:10 speaks of ransom, and vv. 11 and 12 both speak of the Servant's sufferings as being "for many." Thus does Mark identify Jesus, the Son of Man of whom Daniel spoke, with the faithful Servant of God of whom Isaiah spoke.[10]

End Frame or Inclusion:
Jesus Gives Sight to a Blind Man

46 **They came to Jericho.** As he and his disciples and a large crowd were **leaving Jericho, Bartimaeus** son of Timaeus, a blind beggar,

was sitting by the roadside. [47]When he heard that it was Jesus of Nazareth, he began to shout out and say, "**Jesus, Son of David, have mercy on me!**" [48]Many sternly ordered him to be quiet, but he cried out even more loudly, "Son of David, have mercy on me!" [49]Jesus stood still and said, "Call him here." And they called the blind man, saying to him, "Take heart; get up, he is calling you." [50]So **throwing off his cloak**, he sprang up and came to Jesus. [51]Then Jesus said to him, "**What do you want me to do for you?**" The blind man said to him, "**My teacher**, let me see again." [52]Jesus said to him, "Go; your faith has made you well." Immediately he regained his sight **and followed him on the way**.

The journey is all but ended. At its commencement, the disciples were blind. They are still blind, more blind than they were at the start. Jesus is failing. Mark began with a story of the curing of blindness. He finishes with another story of a blind man given sight, and he thus asserts that despite everything Jesus *will* bring the disciples to see.

Mark gives to the blind man a nickname, a composite of Aramaic and Latin transliterated into Greek. As he explains, *Bar* means "son of"; *Timaeus* is akin to the Latin verb *timeo,* "I fear."[11] His name is "son of fear," and the man's wearing a cloak in Jericho, which is warm in winter and unbearably hot in summer, symbolizes that fear. When Mark emphasizes a garment, the garment usually symbolizes something about that person. Jesus' presence lifts him out of that fear. Besides calling Jesus "teacher," the title that appears most frequently in Mark, he also calls him "Son of David." In speaking thus, he identifies Jesus as the Christ, for "son of David" means that. The title is apposite as Jesus approaches at last David's city. Bartimaeus is a blind man who is perceptive, another of Mark's outsiders who are really insiders. His cry for mercy has found a place in the Mass—*Christe eleison.* Jesus hears his plea. Bartimaeus first throws off his cloak, the fear that weighs him down. His sight regained, he becomes a disciple. He follows Jesus along the way.

NOTES

1. The phrase *opisō mou* does mean "behind me" as it is translated, but Mark means specifically, "where a follower should be." In the very next verse, Mark uses the identical phrase *opisō mou* when Jesus says, "if anyone would come *after me.*"

2. We take this to refer to an event that is (1) a long way off yet, but (2) not so far off that everybody now alive will be dead before it happens. Some have argued from this phrase that Mark (and Jesus, perhaps) expected the end of the world to be imminent. It does not have to mean that at all. Semitic expressions are often colorful and sometimes riddlesome. When Saddam Hussein referred to the coming Gulf War as the "mother of all wars" he was using a phrase that has apparently no logical meaning; and yet everyone knew what he meant.

In Luke's Gospel a would-be disciple of Jesus wants permission to bury his father first. We think that means that his father is dead but not yet buried. In that context, Jesus' "Leave the dead to bury their dead" seems to be utterly insensitive; but that is because we misunderstand the expression. William Barclay in his popular commentary on Luke gives an instance of a Middle Easterner who had won a scholarship to Cambridge (*The Daily Study Bible, Revised Edition, The Gospel of Luke* [Edinburgh: St. Andrews Press, 1975], 131). He had the opportunity of either taking up the scholarship immediately or deferring it. He decided to defer the scholarship until "after I have buried my father." His father was still in his late forties and in good health. The Lucan passage is dealt with very clearly in Kenneth E. Bailey, *Through Peasant Eyes* (Grand Rapids, Mich.: William B. Eerdmans, 1980), 26. Bailey quotes an Arab scholar, Ibn al-Salibi. "If his father had really died, why then was he not at that very moment keeping vigil over the body of his father? In reality he intends to defer the matter of following Jesus to a distant future when his father dies as an old man, who knows when."

3. This possibly echoes Is 6:9–11: "And he [the LORD] said, 'Go and say to this people: "Keep listening and listening, but you will not comprehend; keep looking and looking, but you will not understand." Make the heart of this people hard, stop their ears, and close their eyes, so that they may not look with their eyes, and listen with their ears, and comprehend with their hearts, and turn (be converted) and find healing.' Then I said, 'How long, O Lord?' And he said: 'Until cities lie waste uninhabited, and houses without people, and the land is a desolate waste.'"

4. While there are very many instances in OT of God acting to save on

the third day, only one, Hos 6:2, speaks of God raising up on the third day, "After two days he will revive us; on the third day he will raise us up, that we may live before him." Note that "after two days" and "on the third day" have exactly the same meaning. Talking thus, in parallels, was second nature to the ancient Semites. Even this text does not speak explicitly of raising up *from death*. Hosea was not originally talking about resurrection from the dead. When he wrote, God's people had not yet come to belief in the resurrection of the body. Catholics are often very surprised, dismayed even, when they first learn that belief in life beyond the grave arose very late in Judaism. In fact it is not found clearly stated until the last couple of centuries before Christ. This lack of expectation of life after death becomes even more baffling when it is pointed out that neighboring peoples—most notably the Egyptians, for belief in immortality was the *raison d'être* of the pyramids—believed in life after death. The Jews could not conceive of complete nothingness. Consequently, they believed that after death a person had a shadowy existence in Sheol, the abode of the dead. But there was nothing to look forward to in that shadowy existence. Their coming only very late to a belief in life after death was, in reality, part of God's gift to them. They saw the human being as a whole, and they saw life here as mattering. They were preserved by God from the dualism, endemic to human philosophizing, that would divide the human being into spiritual and material. We believe there is a duality about us, but not the dualism that divides a human being into two beings. When the Jews did move toward the notion of life beyond the grave, that belief had to express itself as resurrection of the dead. Human life without body could not be human.

5. *Gehenna* is an abbreviation of *Ge ben Hinnom*. This was a valley outside Jerusalem, the valley of the son of Hinnom. In this valley, King Ahaz, afraid that Yahweh would not protect the Jews against the might of Assyria, which was on the warpath, offered infants in fiery sacrifice to the god Moloch. King Hezekiah, the son of Ahaz, to desecrate the memory of what his father had done, turned that valley into the rubbish dump for Jerusalem. It was still the rubbish heap in Jesus' time. Because of the everlasting burning of the garbage dump, hell came to be pictured as fire. Another image for hell, "where their worm does not die," owes its origin also to this rubbish heap, which had been there for several centuries when Isaiah 66 was written.

6. While this interpretation, because it makes for coherence, is attractive, it is also ingenious. Interpretations that require a high degree of ingenuity are always suspect. The Gentile Christians would hardly have understood it this way. On the other hand, the problem Mark is address-

ing concerned only the Jewish Christians. Perhaps he was addressing them only here. If this interpretation is not what Mark intended to say, then the straightforward meaning of the three verses is not difficult. What is difficult is finding a unity of thought in vv. 41–50. It is *possible* that Mark was copying an existing text that contained the whole of vv. 38–50. Because of the artificial unity accomplished by the bead-stringing technique, Mark decided to include the whole segment. The student should not, however, subscribe easily to such exegesis. It is blaming the author for the student's problem. Beginners do not have to understand everything.

7. I say "too much can be made." A man couldn't sell his wife as he could sell a cow, but the wife was in a position clearly inferior to that of her husband.

8. This is not the place to examine what Jesus would recommend in today's world of frequent marital breakdown, nor how the church should treat those who are divorced and remarried. Scholars generally accept, from the evidence that the New Testament provides, that Jesus said that marriage is, in God's purpose, a lifelong bond. They are aware also that Paul, who knew and affirmed Jesus' teaching, felt able to make an exception.

9. I am indebted to Eugene LaVerdiere, who in a lecture in Ballarat, Australia, pointed out that the second group had to mean Mark's community.

10. "For the Son of Man came not to be served but to serve, and to give his life a ransom for many." During their days of tribal and seminomadic existence, besides the leadership that belonged to the elders of the tribe, there was another kind of leadership that belonged to the tribe's strong man—and that leader's task was to protect the tribe. The strong man was known as the *goel,* which we translate as "redeemer." If another tribe managed to take some of his tribe captive, it fell to the *goel* to rescue them from captivity. The preferred method was to gather the tribe's warriors, go after the marauders, rescue the captives, and teach the captors a lasting lesson. If that was not feasible, the *goel* might gather what goods or money were needed to buy freedom for the captives. That money was known as the ransom. In the Old Testament, God speaks of himself sometimes as the Redeemer of Israel; that is, he is their Protector-Strong Man. When Jesus calls himself here "a ransom" for many, it is important to remember that he is using imagery. When theology moved away from the picture-world of the Semites, a whole theology of redemption developed from taking literally that word *ransom* which Jesus uses about himself. If he pays a ransom, to whom? The first answer given was "to Satan."

Eventually that answer was found wanting; and a new answer was given: "to God." That understanding led eventually to the "pound of flesh" theory of redemption. Jesus did not pay *anything* to *anyone*. It is picture language.

The fourth Servant Song of Isaiah, from which Mark takes the language of ransom, is itself based on the New Year ritual of Persia. There, in atonement for the sins of his subjects, the king accepted *ritual punishment*. As a result, the New Year could begin with a clean slate. Isaiah was inspired by this ritual to see a servant of God suffering, not ritually but really, to atone for his people's sins.

11. "Son of fear" is one possible meaning of the name Bartimaeus. Given Mark's insistence on giving a proper name, his half-translating it to give it further emphasis, his familiarity with Latin, Rome as the locale of the Gospel, and finally his mentioning the detail about throwing off the cloak (which he surely perceives to have significance), I think that it is most likely Mark's intended meaning. However, it is not the only meaning that has been suggested. Mark may have derived Timaeus from the Greek *timaō*, which means "I honor." In that case Bartimaeus would mean "son of a highly honored person." Mark would then be contrasting the man's name with his present condition. This interpretation leaves the reference to his cloak unexplained. Others have suggested that Timaeus is derived from an Aramaic root word meaning "defiled." In this case, the nickname would explain why he is blind. He is the son of defilement. That creates a problem of its own. Mark has translated half of his name. Why leave the second half untranslated. Greek-speaking people would be far more likely to know the meaning of the Hebrew *Bar* than of Mark's coined Aramaic word *Timaeus*. Incidentally, Hebrew and Aramaic were closely related languages, about as close as Italian is to Spanish. Aramaic and Hebrew are sometimes described as being first cousins.

CHAPTER 7

MARK 11:1–12:44
JESUS' MINISTRY IN JERUSALEM

THE MESSIAH ENTERS HIS CITY
(11:1–25)

The Coming Kingdom of Our Ancestor David

When they were approaching Jerusalem, at Bethphage and Bethany, near the Mount of Olives, he sent two of his disciples ²and said to them, "Go into the village ahead of you, and immediately as you enter it, you will find tied there a colt that has never been ridden; untie it and bring it. ³If anyone says to you, 'Why are you doing this?' just say this, 'The Lord needs it and will send it back here immediately.'" ⁴They went away and found a colt tied near a door, outside in the street. As they were untying it, ⁵some of the bystanders said to them, "What are you doing, untying the colt?" ⁶They told them what Jesus had said; and they allowed them to take it. ⁷Then they brought the colt to Jesus and threw their cloaks on it; and he sat on it. ⁸Many people spread their cloaks on the road, and others spread leafy branches that they had cut in the fields. ⁹Then those who went ahead and those who followed were shouting, "Hosanna! Blessed is the one who comes **in the name of the Lord!** ¹⁰**Blessed is the coming kingdom of our ancestor David!** Hosanna in the highest heaven!"

Israel expected that the Messiah would come into the city in triumph from the Mount of Olives. It was also believed that the

Messiah would glorify the Temple (possibly after first purifying it). Mark's account of the entry of Jesus is the account of a divine mess. The entry itself is motley and makeshift, the triumphal steed being requisitioned at the last moment. Those who acclaim Jesus acclaim him wrongly. Jesus had forbidden his disciples to speak of him as the Messiah precisely to avoid expectations about the coming kingdom of David. Moreover, they call him the one who comes in the name of "the Lord." Just before this (v. 3), he has used the title "the Lord" about himself. They still recognize neither Jesus nor the reign of God that he longed to establish. Mark does not translate *Hosanna,* so he expected all of his audience to know its meaning. Most probably, like *Amen* and *Alleluia,* it had already found a place in the Christian liturgy. Literally, *Hosanna* means "Save, Lord," but by the time of Jesus it had become a shout of acclamation.

The instructions Jesus gives (v. 2) suggest supernatural foreknowledge. There will be a similar episode with marked parallels in the preparations for the Last Supper (14:13–14). Mark primarily intends to convey that Jesus is in charge. He may also be getting around a problem created by the way he has structured his narrative. Jesus has not been to Jerusalem previously; yet he has disciples there.

The requisitioning of an animal was a king's prerogative. The requirement that no one had yet ridden on the animal suggests a religious purpose (Jesus enters as king and priest). Kings rode on horses to war. This animal is chosen for a king who enters in peace. The scene evokes Zec 9:9: "Rejoice with all your heart, daughter of Zion! Shout with all your might, daughter of Jerusalem! Behold, your king is coming to you; victorious he is, triumphantly bringing salvation, meekly riding on a donkey, on a colt, the foal of a beast of burden."

The Lord Comes into His Temple

[11]Then he entered Jerusalem and went into the temple; and when he had looked around at everything, as it was already late, he went out to Bethany with the Twelve.

Jesus enters the city to enter the Temple. It is anticlimactic. He enters, looks around, and leaves. The Temple is apparently of little interest to him. It is not the center of *his* world.[1] When Mark wrote, it was obvious to any realistic Jew that the days of the Temple were numbered. Ultimately, there was no possibility that zealots and others holed up in the city of Jerusalem could prevail against the might of the Roman Empire. When Jerusalem fell, the Roman army would so deal with it as to provide a salutary lesson to all other subject peoples, the more so because the Jews had initially been successful in holding on to the city. As things turned out, Titus gave orders that the Temple be preserved from destruction; however, in the general confusion of looting, plundering, and destroying, a burning torch was tossed into the Temple. The sanctuary caught fire and burned down. For some of Mark's audience, the threatened destruction of the Temple was the threatened destruction of the center of their world. Mark wants them to realize that, since Jesus' death, it is not the center. Jesus is their place of meeting with God. He is the foundation of a new, eternal Temple, and that Temple is among them—they are part of it. Just as earlier (7:19) Mark had tried to show them that the dietary laws no longer mattered, so now he tries to steel them against the coming destruction by saying that the Temple is already destroyed. It has served its purpose. Something much better has taken its place.

SANDWICH

Both the stories that follow, while they are events, are primarily symbolic. They are parables in action. There are, in the prophets Jeremiah and Ezekiel, precedents for such symbolic action. Both episodes are a judgment on a leadership that has ensured that this Temple could not be the Temple of the new covenant.

Story 1: Jesus Curses the Fig Tree

[12]On the following day, when they came from Bethany, he was hungry. [13]Seeing in the distance a fig tree in leaf, he went to see

whether perhaps he would find anything on it. When he came to it, he found nothing but leaves, **for it was not the season for figs.** ¹⁴He said to it, "May no one ever eat fruit from you again." And his disciples heard it.

Mark's remark "for it was not the season for figs" gives his audience clear notice that Jesus' action is symbolic. Just what group, though, is Jesus cursing? In the Old Testament, there are numerous instances of the fig, together with the vine, expressing *shalom,* peace and prosperity. However, from the narrative thus far there is no reason at all to suggest that Jesus might be cursing the ordinary people. The precedent for Jesus' cursing is to be found in Jer 8:13: "Thus says the Lord: when I went to the harvest there were no grapes on the vine, nor figs on the fig tree; even the leaves were withered." The ones responsible for this sorry state were the leaders, the teachers of the law, specifically, the scribes. Earlier in the chapter (8:8) Jeremiah had accused them: "How can you say, 'We are wise; ours is the law of the Yahweh,' for it has all been replaced with falsehood by the lying pen of the scribes."

Having condemned by parabolic action the scribes, Jesus goes on to condemn the priestly leadership through a second parable in action.

Story 2: Jesus Closes the Temple

¹⁵Then they came to Jerusalem. And he entered the temple and began to drive out those who were selling and those who were buying in the temple, and he overturned the tables of the money changers and the seats of those who sold doves; ¹⁶and he would not allow anyone to carry (anything) *any vessel* through the temple. ¹⁷He was teaching and saying, "Is it not written, 'My house shall be called **a house of prayer for all the nations**'? But you have made it **a den of robbers.**" ¹⁸And when the chief priests and the scribes heard it, **they kept looking for a way to kill him;** for they were afraid of him, because the whole crowd was spellbound by

his teaching. ¹⁹And when evening came, Jesus and his disciples went out of the city.

By preventing anyone from carrying any vessels through the Temple, Jesus is bringing to a halt the offering of Temple sacrifices. Symbolically he is closing the Temple. He is not glorifying the Temple as was expected. He is not even purifying it. In figure, he is pronouncing its end. Buying and selling animals certified as unblemished and suitable for sacrifice and the changing of money into coinage acceptable for the payment of the Temple tax were both customs of recent origin. Annas, the father-in-law of Caiaphas, had introduced them during his high priesthood.[2] While Jesus, in words taken from Jeremiah (7:11), condemns this practice as exploitative, the heart of Jesus' condemnation lies in the first part, taken from the prophet Isaiah: "My house shall be called **a house of prayer for all the nations.**" Israel, called by God to be a light to the nations, had instead buried itself in self-righteous exclusiveness.[3] In that lay its fundamental failure, and the reason why the universal reign of God could not be founded on it. Every time the church Jesus founded sets out on the path of triumphalism, it is meriting the same condemnation.

Mark links the chief priests and the scribes both in their understanding of Jesus' action and in their determination to kill him. The closing of the Temple and the cursing of the fig tree are then a combined pronouncement that the Temple is finished and Israel's leadership is condemned.

Story 1 Concluded: The Fig Tree Is Withered. What Will Take Its Place?

²⁰In the morning as they passed by, they saw the fig tree withered away to its roots. ²¹Then Peter remembered and said to him, "Rabbi, look! The fig tree that you cursed has withered." The tree has withered.

Just as surely, Jesus' prophetic closing of the Temple will find its fulfillment. What, then, is going to replace it? The answer Jesus gives requires no building at all . . . .

The New Temple

[22]Jesus answered them, "Have faith in God. [23]Truly I tell you, if you say to this mountain, 'Be taken up and thrown into the sea,' and if you do not doubt in your heart, but believe that what you say will come to pass, it will be done for you. [24]So I tell you, whatever you ask for in prayer, believe that you have received it, and it will be yours. [25]Whenever you stand praying, forgive, if you have anything against anyone; so that your Father in heaven may also forgive you your trespasses." [26][*This verse was an interpolation, and is now omitted.*]

Faith in God, prayer, forgiveness—for these, no building is necessary; and in them is all the power we need. When Jesus says, "Have faith!" he is saying, "Though you see the Temple destroyed and Israel bypassed, continue to believe." Once before, when the people of Israel went into exile, the glory of the Lord had left the Temple to accompany them into their exile. Prayer and almsgiving had sufficed in place of the Temple then. So now the impending destruction of the Temple will not mean that the glory of God has left Christ's church.

CONFLICTS IN JERUSALEM
(11:27–12:44)

Jesus' ministry in Galilee had hardly begun when conflict erupted. Mark presented a series of five conflicts (2:1–3:6). Jesus' ministry in Jerusalem had begun with shouts of *Hosanna* and false expectations, as had his ministry in Galilee. Mark presents now a second series of five conflicts.

Conflict 1: Chief Priests, Scribes,
and Elders Challenge Jesus' Authority

[27]Again they came to Jerusalem. As he was walking in the temple, the chief priests, the scribes, and the elders came to him [28]and said, "By what authority are you doing these things? Who gave you this

authority to do them?" ²⁹Jesus said to them, "I will ask you one
question; answer me, and I will tell you by what authority I do
these things. ³⁰Did the baptism of John come from heaven, or was
it of human origin? Answer me." ³¹They argued with one another,
"If we say, 'From heaven,' he will say, 'Why then did you not
believe him?' ³²But shall we say, 'Of human origin'?"—they were
afraid of the crowd, for all regarded John as truly a prophet. ³³So
they answered Jesus, "We do not know." And Jesus said to them,
"Neither will I tell you by what authority I am doing these things."

This episode serves to show Jesus' simple mastery in outwit-
ting the leaders of Israel.

Conflict 2: Jesus Challenges Them:
The Allegory of the Wicked Tenants

^{12:1}Then he began to speak to them in parables. "A man planted a
vineyard, put a fence around it, dug a pit for the wine press, and
built a watchtower; then he leased it to tenants and went to another
country. ²When the season came, he sent a slave to the tenants to
collect from them his share of the produce of the vineyard. ³But they
seized him, and beat him, and sent him away empty-handed. ⁴And
again he sent another slave to them; this one they beat over the
head and insulted. ⁵Then he sent another, and that one they killed.
And so it was with many others; some they beat, and others they
killed. ⁶He had still one other, a beloved son. Finally he sent him to
them, saying, 'They will respect **my son**.' ⁷But those tenants said to
one another, 'This is the heir; come, let us kill him, and the inheri-
tance will be ours.' ⁸So they seized him, killed him, and threw him
out of the vineyard. ⁹What then will the owner of the vineyard do?
He will come and destroy the tenants **and *give* the vineyard to others.** ¹⁰Have you not read this scripture: 'The stone that the builders
rejected has become the cornerstone; ¹¹this was the Lord's doing,
and it is amazing in our eyes'?" ¹²When they realized that he had
told this parable against them, they wanted to arrest him, but they
feared the crowd. So they left him and went away.

In chapter 4, Mark had Jesus explain the parable of the sower by allegorizing it. Here Jesus presents an allegory. It is presumed in the narrative that Mark's audience will know that the arrival of the son makes the tenants think that his father, the owner, has died. Any bystander would have recalled the words of Is 5:1–6:

> Let me sing for my beloved my song about my love's vineyard: My beloved had a vineyard on a very fertile hill. He dug the soil and cleared it of stones, and planted it with choicest of vines; in the midst of it he built a watchtower, and made a winepress for it; he expected it to yield grapes, but all it yielded were wild grapes. And now, inhabitants of Jerusalem and people of Judah, judge between me and my vineyard. What more was there to do for my vineyard than I have done? When I looked for its crop of grapes, why did it yield wild grapes? And now I will tell you what I am going to do to my vineyard. I will remove its hedge, and let it be grazed on; I will knock down its wall, and it shall be trampled. I will leave it a waste; it shall not be pruned or hoed, but overgrown with briars and thorns; and I will give a command to the clouds not to rain any rain upon it.

It is apparent that the chief priests, the scribes, and the elders recognize that they are the unfaithful tenants of the story.[4] And they understand Jesus' threat that they will be destroyed and that the Lord's vineyard will be entrusted to others. (Notice that Jesus does not say *lease* but *give*.) Jesus' appeal to Psalm 118 makes even more obvious his claim to be the Son of God who will be rejected by them yet become the cornerstone. They refuse to listen. They have already decided (11:18) to kill him. His attempt to hold up a mirror to their thoughts only makes them more determined.

By Jesus' describing himself as the cornerstone, Mark has added another dimension to the Temple motif. God is founding a new Temple on his Son. The old has given way to something greater.

Conflict 3: Pharisees and Herodians Seek to Trap Jesus: Taxes to Caesar

[13]Then they sent to him some Pharisees and some Herodians to trap him in what he said. [14]And they came and said to him, "Teacher,

we know that you are sincere, and show deference to no one; for you do not regard people with partiality, but teach the way of God in accordance with truth. Is it lawful to pay taxes to the emperor, or not? [15]Should we pay them, or should we not?" But knowing their hypocrisy, he said to them, "Why are you putting me to the test? Bring me a denarius and let me see it." [16]And they brought one. Then he said to them, "Whose head is this, and whose title?" They answered, "The emperor's." [17]Jesus said to them, "Give to the emperor the things that are the emperor's, and to God the things that are God's." And they were utterly amazed at him.

In this episode, Jesus' mastery is again obvious. On the level of argument, Jesus is the clear winner. However, political power belongs to them, not to him; and they will defeat him. For a third time in the Gospel (3:6; 7:15), unlikely bedfellows are found together, symbols of religious establishment and secular establishment. This episode has been much abused in subsequent history. People have used it to justify an unhealthy separation of the political from the moral—it's got nothing to do with morality; it's politics, or business.

Jesus does not answer their question at all. Instead, he turns the question back on them, revealing that they use Caesar's coinage. His statement "Give back to God what belongs to God" makes no separation between secular and religious, for, and they knew this perfectly well, everything belongs to God.[5]

Conflict 4: Sadducees Seek to Trap Jesus:
The Resurrection of the Dead

[18]Some Sadducees, who say there is no resurrection, came to him and asked him a question, saying, [19]"Teacher, Moses wrote for us that 'if a man's brother dies, leaving a wife but no child, the man shall marry the widow and raise up children for his brother.' [20]There were seven brothers; the first married and, when he died, left no children; [21]and the second married her and died, leaving no children; and the third likewise; [22]none of the seven left children. Last of all the woman herself died. [23]In the resurrection whose wife

will she be? For the seven had married her." ²⁴Jesus said to them, **"Is not this the reason you are wrong, that you know neither the scriptures nor the power of God?** ²⁵For when they rise from the dead, they neither marry nor are given in marriage, but are like angels in heaven. ²⁶And as for the dead being raised, have you not read in the book of Moses, in the story about the bush, how God said to him, 'I am the God of Abraham, the God of Isaac, and the God of Jacob'? ²⁷He is God not of the dead, but of the living; you are quite wrong."[6]

The party favored by the chief and wealthy priestly families was that of the Sadducees. The name is said to come from Zadok, appointed high priest by King David. The party of the Sadducees traced itself back to him. While this lineage is improbable, the Sadducee party may have had quite ancient roots, going back to the exile in Babylon. The Sadducees were the conservative Jews. They accepted the Torah but rejected the more recent writings and doctrinal developments within Judaism. (The first five books of the Old Testament—Genesis, Exodus, Leviticus, Numbers, and Deuteronomy—are collectively described in Judaism as Torah. Christians usually call these five books the Pentateuch.) The Sadducees would correspond to, among Christian groups, those who say "nothing beyond the Bible." They denied the existence of angels. As Mark mentions, they also denied the resurrection of the dead. They throw at Jesus a story they had used many times, no doubt to confound the Pharisees. Jesus' answer cuts the ground from under their argument. He quotes from "the Book of Moses," that is, from Torah, which they accepted.

Not a Conflict: A Scribe Questions Jesus: The Great Commandment

²⁸One of the scribes came near and heard them disputing with one another, and seeing that he answered them well, he asked him, "Which commandment is the first of all?" ²⁹Jesus answered, "The first is, 'Hear, O Israel: the Lord our God, the Lord is one; ³⁰you shall love the Lord your God with all your heart, and with all your

soul, and with all your mind, and with all your strength.' [31]The second is this, 'You shall love your neighbor as yourself.' There is no other commandment greater than these." [32] Then the scribe said to him, "You are right, Teacher; you have truly said that 'he is one, and besides him there is no other'; [33]and 'to love him with all the heart, and with all the understanding, and with all the strength,' and 'to love one's neighbor as oneself,'—this is much more important than all whole burnt offerings and sacrifices." [34]When Jesus saw that he answered wisely, he said to him, "You are not far from the kingdom of God." After that no one dared to ask him any question.

Mark surprises us now with another outsider to the story, and one whom we would presume to be malevolent toward Jesus, who is really an insider, "not far from the kingdom of God." Mark deflates our smug self-righteousness (We are on Jesus' side. We are not like them.) In the time of Jesus, partly because exaggerated legalism had proliferated to such an extent as to be debilitating, the rabbis were asking, "What, among all this, really matters?" The answer Jesus gave was all too obvious. Called the *Shema Israel,* the first part of Jesus' answer was recited by Jews every day. Jesus was probably not the first to say that this was the greatest commandment. He is unique, however, in placing next to the *Shema* the additional commandment "You shall love your neighbor as yourself."

Mark further develops his Temple theology. The imminent destruction of the Temple in Jerusalem will mean the loss of the whole body of Jewish sacrificial ritual. This scribe sees that sacrificial ritual is *not* the highest religious value; and Jesus agrees with him.[7]

Jesus Poses a Question: Messiah—Son of David and Lord of David?

[35]While Jesus was teaching in the temple, he said, "How can the scribes say that the Messiah is the son of David? [36]David himself, by the Holy Spirit, declared, 'The Lord said to my Lord, "Sit at my

right hand, until I put your enemies under your feet."' [37]David himself calls him Lord; so how can he be his son?" And the large crowd was listening to him with delight.

Jesus takes the initiative in this final conflict story. He brings up a poser, for which none of his hearers can provide an answer. Jesus is quoting from Psalm 110, one of the psalms of David.[8] Right order demands that the son cannot be placed above the father. The Messiah is to be David's son; yet David calls him, "My Lord." Jesus is inviting his hearers to take a second look at him. They refuse. The die is cast.

Jesus Condemns the Scribes

[38]As he taught, he said, "Beware of the scribes, who like to walk around in long robes, and to be greeted with respect in the marketplaces, [39]and to have the best seats in the synagogues and places of honor at banquets! [40]They devour widows' houses and for the sake of appearance say long prayers. They will receive the greater condemnation."

Jesus will soon have judgement pronounced on him. Before he faces his passion, he wishes to warn the people against their scribes. His warning is also an invitation to the scribes to repent. It is a prophetic warning. The particular example Mark chooses leads into the final cameo of Jesus' ministry in Jerusalem, and his ministry among God's chosen people.

The End of Jesus' Ministry in the Temple: The Widow Who Gave All

[41]He sat down opposite the treasury, and watched the crowd putting money into the treasury. Many rich people put in large sums. [42]A poor widow came and put in two small copper coins,

which are worth a penny. [43]Then he called his disciples and said to them, "Truly I tell you, this poor widow has put in more than all those who are contributing to the treasury. [44]For all of them have contributed out of their abundance; but she out of her poverty has put in everything she had, all she had to live on."

Some scholars, among them liberation theologians, have read into this episode a condemnation of a religious system that put such expectations on the destitute widow. As such, it would be simply an illustration of the condemnation Jesus has just spoken. While I do not want to be identified with those who spurn liberation theology, I cannot see that this is Mark's theology here.[9] The widow illustrates rather what a scribe had only recently spoken, "You are right, Teacher; you have truly said that 'he is one, and beside him there is no other'; and 'to love him with all the heart, and with all the understanding, and with all the strength,' and 'to love one's neighbor as oneself' is much more important than all whole burnt offerings and sacrifices." The widow's worthless offering speaks mightily the *Shema Israel* that she prayed each morning and night.

Mark has drawn here a three-way tension, a scribe, a widow, the scribes. A scribe had shown that the reign of God might have come about through Jesus' ministry. Yet, as a class, the scribes had contradicted God's purpose. The scribes copied and interpreted Torah, the law. For that, they were meant to receive no remuneration. Like the rabbis and all Jewish men, they were meant to keep themselves by working at a trade. However, the honor shown them—at banquets they took precedence over rabbis and even over parents—had turned their heads. Some had found for themselves lucrative work through exploiting extracurricular opportunities that came their way. The case Jesus gives came about because widows, being women, were considered unfit to manage their husbands' estates. The scribes could find work as trustees; and, like many trustees in our time too, they so managed affairs as to enrich themselves. Mark has presented us with a scribe, and a widow, each of whom were ready to embrace the reign of God. In contrast with them the scribal class, custodians of Torah, are a guarantee that the reign of God will not come from God's people accepting God's Messiah. It must come then through his accepting rejection.

The story of the widow's mite is the final event of Jesus' ministry. It is an event, and it is a parable of Jesus. In her poverty, the widow has placed all in God's hands. Jesus, in the utter poverty of his failure, having lived in his own life the acceptance of God's reign that he preached, is about to make that surrender to God complete. He who lived each day by the *Shema Israel* and who has, in the words of the Letter to the Hebrews, learned obedience through suffering, now, in accepting rejection fully and surrendering himself to the will of his enemies, is to be made perfect. That widow, in accepting completely the risk of depending on God, is a paradigm of Jesus himself. One more outsider, she mirrors the very heart of God.

NOTES

1. Mark interweaves into the Jerusalem ministry and the passion much material about the Temple: 11:12–25 (especially vv. 16, 17a, 17b); 12:1–12 (especially vv. 10b–11); 12:38–44 (especially v. 33); 12:41–44; 13:1–37; 14:58; 15:29b–30; 15:38 all deal with the destruction of the Temple and its replacement.

2. Annas was followed in the office of high priest by five of his sons, and then by Caiaphas. The house of Annas controlled the high priesthood for several decades. While the buying and selling was ostensibly to help pilgrims, it was in fact a racket, lucrative for those engaged in commerce and for the Temple. The prices were exorbitant, exploitative. Later Jewish writings speak with disgust about the house of Annas. In view of this, it is curious that some Christian scholars still peddle the theory that the Romans were the prime movers in executing Jesus, and the Gospels transfer the blame to the Sanhedrin in order to exonerate the Romans and, of course, to legitimize Christianity. There is nothing anti-Semitic in claiming that the house of Annas was ruthless enough to be willing to legally murder someone whose influence they feared.

Pagans were allowed into the first court of the Temple, but no further. The booths for buying and selling were set up in this area, making it impossible for anyone to pray there. Consequently, the Gentiles were deprived of any place of prayer in the Temple.

3. There is a tension in later Old Testament writings between the need of Judaism to protect itself from the corrupting influence of the world outside, and the call to be the light of that world outside, to reveal Yahweh to it. The tension is visible in the later writings. Sadly, the exclusivist ideal won; so much so that, in the Greco-Roman world, the antipathy between Jew and Gentile was seen as the archetype of all human conflicts. The books of Ezra and Nehemiah illustrate the exclusivist tendency. The books of Ruth and of Jonah illustrate the universalist tendency.

4. The chief priests were quite wealthy and owned land in Galilee which they leased out to tenants. Along with other landowners, they exploited their tenants. In Jesus' allegory, the instincts of the audience lead them to identify with the landowner, but soon they realize that he is tracing a history of the perfidy of Israel's leaders, shown in their treatment of the prophets. Likewise they realize that Jesus is identifying himself with the Son, the last one God will send them. They know that Jesus is claiming to be God's only Son, but they cannot believe that. Jesus' quotation from Psalm 118 spells out more clearly still the choice confronting them. The targums (popular Aramaic paraphrases of the scriptures) identified the builders as the scribes, who reject the *talya* (= son *or* lamb), who nevertheless becomes leader and ruler. The targums generally were much more than free translations. They interpreted, embroidered, and embellished the text (see Ralph Martin, *Mark, Evangelist and Theologian* [Grand Rapids, Mich.: Zondervan, 1973], 194).

5. The Herodians naturally supported the payment of the tribute. Herod's authority depended on the goodwill of the emperor. The Pharisees, while they regarded the presence of the Romans as an outrage, thought it better not to make an issue of it, provided that the Romans left them free to practice their religion.

6. It may come as a surprise that the law of Moses sometimes required bigamy. Remember that, at the time of Moses, and for many centuries afterwards, the Jews did not believe in life after death. A man's name lived on in his children. To preserve a man's name from extinction, if he died childless, his brother had to marry his wife and conceive children for his dead brother. Thus he would have two wives. The law was known as the levirate law. It is thought that, by the time of Jesus, it had fallen into disuse.

7. Jesus' sacrifice was *not* a ritual sacrifice, though it becomes present

to *us* through a ritual, the Eucharist. In Jesus' life and death, the love command and sacrifice each found their perfect expression and became one. The language of ritual sacrifice, applied to Jesus, is picture language.

The reality of Jesus is far deeper than any ritual language can convey. The blessing that Jesus, as head of the home, pronounced over the bread and wine was, on a household level, not unlike the blessing that the priest in the Temple pronounced over the Communion or full sacrifices. This prayer of thanksgiving, called the *Todah*, seems to have developed out of the Jews' contact (during the exile in Babylon) with Persian religious practice. Eventually, the *Todah* came to be regarded as the most important part of the rite of full sacrifice. The sacrifice came to be called the Sacrifice of Praise. See Philippe Béguerie and Claude Duchesneau, *How to Understand the Sacraments* (London: SCM Press, 1991), 85.

8. Modern scholars hold that David did not in fact write this Psalm. This does not matter. In Jesus' day David was perceived as the author. Jesus points out the difficulty that this poses. He is not looking for someone to suggest that David did not write the Psalm. He wants them to see that the Messiah, the son of David, is *more* than they were expecting.

9. The widow's mite has, nevertheless, for nearly two thousand years been used by wealthy people to justify their meanness; and this is a part of the system of oppression, liberation from which is, according to liberation theologians, a necessary aspect of God's salvation. The first to suggest that this episode is presented by Mark as a condemnation of the religious system was Addison Wright (who is not a liberation theologian), in "The Widow's Mite: Praise or Lament? A Matter of Context,"*Catholic Biblical Quarterly* (1982): 256.

CHAPTER 8

MARK 13:1–37
THE ESCHATOLOGICAL
DISCOURSE

The ministry of Jesus is complete. He is about to face his passion, to be put to the test. But Mark pauses now for this quite different scene, in which he changes key to present Jesus pointing his disciples toward the future.

The title of this chapter may sound frightening. "Discourse" means simply a talk. Except for the introductory setting, and two questions from the disciples, the whole chapter is a talk given by Jesus. "Eschatological" means "about the last things." This title is not completely accurate. The talk is not exclusively about the end.

Sometimes the chapter is called the Apocalyptic Discourse or the Little Apocalypse because, in a large part of the discourse, Jesus employs the language of *apocalyptic*. The language of apocalyptic is not literal, but symbolic. To read it literally is to read it wrongly. To seek literal fulfillment, as many do, is to misunderstand the nature of apocalyptic. Mark has employed the imagery of apocalyptic briefly on one earlier occasion (8:38–9:1). He will employ it later, again briefly, in his account of Jesus' passion (14:62; 15:33). Each time Mark's concern is to identify the fulfillment of the prophecy of Daniel about the Son of Man. He could, with no difficulty at all, have seen Daniel's prophecy about the coming of the Son of Man with great power and glory fulfilled in Jesus' resurrection. But Mark has seen more deeply than that. He sees Daniel 7 fulfilled in Jesus' crucifixion. (Of course, if Jesus had not risen, it would not have occurred to Mark to see Jesus' death as glory, power, or sovereignty, nor as the revelation of God. Neither would he be writing a Gospel.)

To us, apocalyptic is a strange word. It wasn't so strange to Mark's Christians of the first century. Compared with most apocalyptic—for example, with the New Testament book called the Apocalypse or book of Revelation, Mark's apocalyptic is mild, even pale. The word *Apocalypse* is derived from a Greek word that means "revelation." Apocalyptic segments in chapter 13 will be underlined. The important thing to remember is that this vivid language is not meant to be understood literally.

Another important aspect of apocalyptic is the collapsing of time. The reader can be taken back and forth through time without any clear indications. Mark employs this technique. In addition, the predictions made in apocalyptic can have multiple fulfillments, indeed even perennial fulfillment. One prediction may predict more than one thing.[1]

13:1As he **came out of the temple**, one of his disciples said to him, "Look, Teacher, what large stones and what large buildings!" 2Then Jesus asked him, "Do you see these great buildings? Not one stone will be left here upon another; all will be thrown down." 3When he was sitting on the Mount of Olives opposite the temple, Peter, James, John, and Andrew asked him **privately**, 4"Tell us, when will **these things** be, and what will be **the sign** that **all these things are about to be accomplished?"**

This initial segment is not apocalyptic. Jesus is leaving, departing finally from the Temple. The disciples express wonder at the Temple. Jesus says that it will all be pulled down, stone by stone. (The disciples ask when "these things" will take place. We would expect a singular "this thing," but the Temple was not one but several buildings.) In recording this, Mark is telling his fellow Jewish Christians in Rome, panic-stricken at the thought that the center of their world was about to disappear, that Jesus had said that it would happen. The Temple in Jerusalem has served its purpose. God has already given to us a new and better Temple. Mark is continuing his Temple theology, which he began to develop when Jesus entered the city.

The four apostles ask Jesus privately. Jesus' teaching had been addressed initially to the crowds. As he accepted his failure with the leadership and the crowds, he began to concentrate on teaching the disciples. He knows now that even his disciples have been unable to understand him. He entrusts this final and difficult teaching not to all his disciples, nor even to the Twelve, but only to Peter, James, John, and Andrew. Jesus is reduced to trying to bring these four, the first to have been called by him, to see. They ask Jesus two questions: (1) When will these things be? (2) What will be the sign that **all** these things are about to be accomplished? Reading on from v. 4, Jesus seems to ignore their questions. He does answer them, but only much later.

Notice that they ask for a sign. In chapter 8, the Pharisees asked for a sign, and Jesus condemned them. Some interpreters see the disciples condemning themselves by asking here what the sign would be. This is not the case. Jesus has not been slow in rebuking his disciples when rebuke is needed, but he expresses no rebuke here.

They ask Jesus for the sign, not of *these things*—that is, the destruction of the Temple—but of *all these things*. The disciples presume that the destruction of the Temple presages the collapse of everything. Thus, their interpretation of Jesus' statement introduces the theme of the last things. Eschatology is derived from a Greek word *eschaton,* which means the "last thing." Apocalyptic symbolism was usually employed to speak of the last things. Mark is going to tell his readers that the destruction of the Temple will by no means be the end of everything.

This second request then takes the discussion into the arena of eschatology and of apocalyptic. Mark is going to deal here with three interrelated events: (1) the end of the world, (2) the coming of the Son of Man, and (3) the destruction of the Temple.[2]

1. *The end of the world.* Mark's purpose through the chiasm given below is to state explicitly that the end is *not* imminent. The gospel must first be preached to all the nations.

2. *The coming of the Son of Man.* Our natural instinct is to identify this with the end of the world. The parousia *will* be the ending of the world. (*Parousia,* like *eschaton,* is a Greek word. It is often used to signify Jesus' coming in glory to complete the world

by raising us from the dead and sitting in judgment.) That identification is not wrong; however, it is not primary. The coming of
the Son of Man is on Calvary. Mark has once already (8:38–9:1)
identified Jesus' naming of himself as the Son of Man with the
destiny foretold for the Son of Man in Daniel 7. Mark is eager to
state that the destiny of Daniel's Son of Man is fulfilled already in
Jesus. Jesus will identify himself very explicitly in the terms of Dn
7:13–14 as he stands (14:62), bound and helpless, before the
Sanhedrin. The coming of the Son of Man in power and glory
happens on the cross. I repeat what I stated earlier, because it is
central to Mark's theology and his most important contribution
to the New Testament: Mark, very easily and with complete plausibility, could have identified the fulfillment of the prophecy of
Daniel 7 with Jesus' resurrection. The very fact that Mark identified the man crucified, utterly lacking in either power or dignity,
as the Son of Man coming with power and great glory must give
us pause. It is the completely unexpected revelation of God.

3. *The destruction of the Temple.* Once again, we think explicitly of 70 C.E., and we are not wrong. However, it also is fulfilled
first of all in Jesus' death, as we shall see in due course.

At v. 5 Mark begins a chiasm. As explained earlier, in a chiasm
the center is the key for interpreting the whole. Because of the
calamities that have befallen the community, some of the members of Mark's community believed that the end of the world
could not be far off.[3] Mark has Jesus assert that the end will not
come until the gospel has been preached to all the nations. This
message is reinforced by "the end is not yet" (v. 7); and "this is
but the beginning of the birthpangs" (v. 8). Birthpangs hardly
speak ending.

Concentric Structure or Chiasm[4]

A: *False Prophets (13:5–6)*

[5]Then Jesus began to say to them, "Beware that no one leads you
astray. [6]Many will come (in) *assuming* my name and say, 'I AM
(he)!' and they will lead many astray.

The ones claiming to speak in Jesus' name are impostors. That is clearly the meaning of the Greek. Some impostors say, "I am." Translators add "he" to "I am," and that is legitimate. These impostors will be claiming to be Christ. However, the Greek is simply *egō eimi*, "I AM"; and, in view of the meaning of *ego eimi* in 6:50 (an assertion of Jesus' divinity), Mark possibly intends an assertion of Jesus' divinity here too.

In addition, in claiming to be Christ, the impostors are claiming also to be inaugurating the end of the world. However, from available historical evidence we do not know of any people who, in those early years of the church, actually claimed to be Jesus returned.

B: Wars and Rumors of Wars
(13:7–8)

[7]When you hear of <u>wars and rumors of wars</u>, do not be alarmed; this must take place, but **the end is** (still to come) *not yet.* [8]For <u>nation will rise against nation, and kingdom against kingdom;</u> there will be <u>earthquakes</u> in various places; there will be <u>famines.</u> **This is but the beginning of the birth pangs**.

This is apocalyptic language. The constant temptation is to take it literally and to look for its fulfillment in particular events. In 63 C.E. Pompeii was largely destroyed by an earthquake. There were earthquakes in Italy in 68 C.E. There were also famines in parts of the empire. The empire was experiencing wars as rival armies fought to have their candidate installed as emperor. These events fulfill these verses, but such predictions are being fulfilled perennially, in every age. The language is picture language, symbolic of all troubles, disasters, and catastrophes. When will they happen? They happen constantly. How should we read them? As portents of the end? No, they are signs of life, not death: birth pangs, not death throes.

C: Actual Christian Experience
of Suffering (13:9)

[9]"As for yourselves, beware; for they will hand you over to councils; and you will be beaten in synagogues; and you will stand

before governors and kings because of me, as a testimony to them.

Mark gives examples here from the experience of Christians in various places, persecution by both Jews and pagans. Remember that Jesus is talking about constant persecutions. St. Paul is an outstanding example of the fulfillment of this in the life of the early church.

D: Center: The World Is Not Going to End Just Yet (13:10)

[10]And the good news must first be proclaimed to all nations.

As the center, this is Mark's key message. It is, implicitly a command to proclaim the Good News to all nations.[5] Moreover, it implies that a significant group in Mark's community believed that the end of the world was at hand. They may have been filled with expectant joy, or they may have been filled with dread, seeing their world collapsing. Either way, they are being distracted from their task.

C1: Actual Christian Experience of Suffering (13:11–13)

[11]When they bring you to trial and hand you over, do not worry beforehand about what you are to say; but say whatever is given you at that time, for it is not you who speak, but **the Holy Spirit**. [12]Brother will betray brother to death, and a father his child, and children will rise against parents and have them put to death; [13]and you will be hated by all because of my name. But the one who endures to the end will be saved.

The advice in v. 11 is for all being persecuted for the gospel. Sometimes chapter 13 is called "The passion of the church."

Before Jesus goes to his passion, he talks about the passion of those who take up their cross and follow after him.

Jesus never promised that fidelity to the gospel would make life a bed of roses. Indeed, their basking in the resurrection while forgetting the cross, together with their reliance on *self* instead of on *the Holy Spirit*, had brought about their failure in the persecution. Similarly, the failure of Jesus' chosen Twelve (to be made complete in his passion) had been due to their self-reliance.

Mark's audience were still feeling the humiliating pain of "brother will betray brother to death." Just as Peter was sure that he would never deny Jesus, so the Christians in Rome had been sure of their basic loyalty to one another.

B1: Wars and Rumors of Wars
(13:14–20)

[14]"But when you see the desolating sacrilege set up where it ought not to be (let the reader understand), then those in Judea must flee to the mountains; [15]the one on the housetop must not go down or enter the house to take anything away; [16]the one in the field must not turn back to get a coat. [17]Woe to those who are pregnant and to those who are nursing infants in those days! [18]Pray that it may not be in winter. [19]For in those days there will be **suffering, such as has not been from the beginning of the creation that God created until now, no, and never will be again**. [20]And if the Lord had not cut short those days, no one would be saved; but for the sake of **the elect, whom he chose**, he has cut short those days."

The parallel segment (B, 13:7–8) spoke about troubles throughout the empire. B1 deals particularly with the troubles in Judea. The consequences of Judea's revolt against Rome are the subject of Mark's message here. The urgent intensity of the language is Semitic picture hyperbole.

At the time Mark wrote, the troubles consequent on the revolt of 66 C.E. were already being experienced. A technique used commonly with apocalyptic is to prophesy, from a point in the past, a future that has already happened at the time of writing. No deception is involved. The readers of apocalyptic understood the technique.

"The Desolating Sacrilege" is an apocalyptic image borrowed from Dn 9:27, "He shall make a strong covenant with many for the space of one week, and for space of one half of one week he shall prevent any sacrifice from being offered; and above all these abominations he shall bring the **Abomination of Desolation**, until the ruin that is decreed is poured out upon the destroyer." In the book of Daniel, the Abomination of Desolation referred to a definite event, the turning of the Temple of Yahweh into a pagan shrine by the erection there of the altar of Zeus (1 Mc 1:54). Here the desolating sacrilege is, in the first place, Jesus' being condemned by the Sanhedrin, the guardian of the Temple.[6] The keepers of the Temple have condemned the Lord of the Temple. The rest of this segment is also, then, talking (apocalyptically) first of all about the cataclysmic, catastrophic significance of the condemning of the Son of God to death.

It refers also to another event that helped to bring about the Temple's destruction. Mark's "let the reader understand" implies that they know what he is referring to because it has already happened. Most likely the sacrilege Mark referred to was the taking over of the Temple by the Zealots in 66 C.E. In that context, the suffering spoken of is the suffering of Judea at the hands of the Romans. Its being called the worst that would ever happen is Semitic hyperbole. The extreme language of v. 19 is borrowed from Dn 21:1.

A1: False Prophets (13:21–23)

[21]"And if anyone says to you at that time, 'Look! Here is the Messiah!' or 'Look! There he is!'—do not believe it. [22] False messiahs and false prophets will appear and produce signs and omens, to lead astray, if possible, **the elect**.[7] [23]But be alert; I have already told you everything."

As previously with A (13:5–6), people are falsely announcing the parousia. Once again, while in the period of turmoil over the decades that led to the revolt of Judea in 66 C.E. we know of many revolutionary leaders, we do not know for certain that any actually were designated as Messiah.

The talk here and earlier (v. 20) of the "elect" smacks of predestination. Once again it is an example of the Semitic way of thinking. It did not suggest what we think of as Calvinist predestination either to Mark, or to his audience (see 4:10–12).[8]

[24]"But in **those** days, after that suffering, <u>the sun will be darkened, and the moon</u> will <u>not give its light,</u> [25]<u>and the stars will be falling from heaven, and the powers in the heavens will be shaken.</u>[9] [26]Then they will see <u>'the Son of Man coming in clouds'</u> with great power and glory. [27]<u>Then he will send out the angels, and gather his elect from the four winds, from the ends of the earth to the ends of heaven.</u> [28]From the fig tree learn its lesson: as soon as its branch becomes tender and puts forth its leaves, you know that summer is near. [29]So also, when you see these things taking place, **you know that he is near,** at the very gates. [30]**Truly I tell you, this generation will not pass away until all these things have taken place.** [31]Heaven and earth will pass away, but my words will not pass away."

Verse 24, in saying "in **those** days, after that suffering," seems to be placing the coming of the Son of Man *after* the destruction of the Temple; but it gives no indication at all whether it will be immediately after, soon after, a long time after, or whatever. Remember that, in apocalyptic, time is collapsed. At one level the events that will come "after that suffering" are about the end of the world. The descriptions "the sun will be darkened" are apocalyptic imagery. The parousia is being spoken of. Fundamentally, however, these verses describe another event much nearer in time to Jesus' speaking. If the Desolating Sacrilege is primarily the condemnation of Jesus, then the sun being darkened will be fulfilled on Calvary, and the coming of the Son of Man with great power and glory will take place on the afternoon of Good Friday. The cry of the centurion will acknowledge that. And, from Calvary, Jesus' angels, his messengers, evangelists (the Greek *angelos* means "messenger") will go out to preach the gospel to the four corners of the earth, gathering God's elect.

In the course of the narrative of Jesus' ministry, Mark has prepared us to so interpret Calvary.

We have already heard Jesus speak of coming in power: "Those who are ashamed of me and of my words in this adulterous and sinful generation, of them **the Son of Man** will also be ashamed **when he comes** in the **glory** of his Father with the holy **angels**" (Mk 8:38–39). And he said to them, "Truly I tell you, there are some standing here who will not taste death until they see that the kingdom of God has come with **power.**" These verses speak about the parousia; but they are fulfilled immediately in the Transfiguration, and primarily on Calvary. Mark has already (10:35–40) stated very deliberately that Jesus comes in **glory** at Calvary.

This is an example of the apocalyptic collapsing of time. Three events, not simultaneous, are spoken of simultaneously.

[32]"But about **that** day or hour **no one knows, neither the angels in heaven, nor the Son, but only the Father.**[10]

[33]Beware, keep alert; for you do not know when the time will come. [34]It is like a man going on a journey, when he leaves home and puts his slaves in charge, each with his work, and commands the doorkeeper to be on the watch. [35]Therefore, keep awake—for you do not know when the master of the house will come, in the evening, or at midnight, or at cockcrow, or at dawn, [36]or else he may find you asleep when he comes suddenly. [37]And what I say to you I say to all: **Keep awake.**"

The hour spoken of here is Jesus' coming in glory at the end of the world. To some it comes as a shock that Jesus professes ignorance of the time. That results from not taking seriously enough God's Son becoming human. To be human is to possess only limited knowledge. More noteworthy is the ranking Jesus gives to himself here: he, the Son, is above the angels. The same verse that is not ashamed to acknowledge the limitations that come from Jesus' being human also asserts the absolute uniqueness, the divinity, of this human being, the Son. The eschatological hour is, however, much more imminent than that coming. Just as Jesus, in the parable that concludes the discourse, gives three times the exhortation, "Stay awake, alert," so, at Gethsemane, he will again speak three times about staying awake. And there he will face the eschatological hour, before which he will shrink. The exhortation is another example of collapsed time. It means, "be ready for the end, the parousia." Yet its meaning is also immediate. In Gethsemane the apostles, bidden to keep awake with Jesus, will go to sleep and will not be ready. The exhortation is not just for them, however, any more than it is just for the end. It is an enduring command for all of us all the time: Stay awake, don't give up!

Mark 13 is reckoned as being the most commented on text in the whole of the New Testament. That is surely evidence enough of the commentators' hesitations and uncertainties about parts of this chapter. If the reader feels somewhat ill at ease with some parts of this chapter, so do those who are much better qualified than us to exegete it.

To sum up the message of chapter 13: (1) Living the gospel will always be a battle. At no stage, while time endures, will we be able to say, "the time for suffering is over." (2) Jesus is victorious. He, the Son of Man of Dn 7:13–14, has come on the clouds of heaven on the cross. When he comes at the end, his victory will be manifest; but the decisive battle has already taken place. It took place on Calvary. (3) The Temple **will** be destroyed. Jesus prophesied it, but that is not the end of the world. It is rather the beginning. (4) Troubles do not mean that the end is near. They are the pains of birth, signs of hope; so don't give up. Jesus makes it clear that the church will have its passion. Yet he says to us: "Do not be alarmed . . . do not worry . . . the Holy Spirit in you . . . the beginning of the birthpangs . . . know that he is near, at the very gates . . . Heaven and Earth will pass away, but my words will not pass away." Jesus would sustain us in hope.[11]

Excursus 4
Did Jesus Prophesy the Temple's
Destruction?

Some commentators think that Jesus did not foretell the destruction of
the Temple, and that Mark is prophesying after the event. Exegesis of this
sort arises from a desire to remove from the Gospels any trace of the
supernatural. Five hundred years earlier, the prophet Jeremiah forecast
the destruction of the previous Temple, the Temple of Solomon. Jeremiah's prophecy was fulfilled. In 63 C.E., a visionary in Jerusalem loudly
proclaimed that the Temple was going to be destroyed. The Jewish
authorities wanted him jailed, but the Roman procurator ruled that he
was insane and harmless. In the event, the visionary perished in the
destruction of the city in 70 C.E.

I have no difficulty accepting that Jesus did prophesy the destruction
of the Temple. If it is objected that Christians were not generally aware
of the prophecy, that is precisely the way it is with prophecy. It doesn't
become obvious until near the event. Mark, writing not long before the
Temple's destruction, guessed wrongly some of the details of the destruction. He has Jesus say that the sanctuary will be torn down stone by
stone. In fact, it was accidentally set on fire and burned down. This error
in detail helps to date Mark's Gospel. If Mark had written after the
Temple had been destroyed in 70 C.E., it is argued, he would have corrected the error. While this argument has some weight, it is not apodic-
tic. The Gospel of Luke, which is generally said to have been written
about 85 C.E., well after the destruction of the Temple, employs in one
place (21:6) language similar to Mark's language here—not one stone left
upon another. But in another part of his Apocalyptic Discourse (21:20),
Luke so describes the fate of Jerusalem that he almost certainly has been
influenced by what actually took place. Mark says that the Temple will be
pulled down. As well, he does not say anything about the destruction of
the city. It does seem that Mark wrote before the events of 70 C.E.

Among the scholars, while there is still strong disagreement about dat-
ing the Gospel before or after the destruction of the Temple, each side of
the debate places the writing shortly *before* or shortly *after* 70 C.E. In the
scenario I have presented, it makes little difference which of these is true.
The essential element is turmoil among Mark's Roman Judeo-Christians
over the fall of the city and Temple. I opt for *before* 70 C.E. simply because
I do not sense that Mark is writing with the benefit of hindsight.

NOTES

1. Prediction is sometimes, but by no means always, a part of prophecy. It is important to understand that the essential task of the prophet is to speak for God. In modern parlance, prophecy has come to mean simply predicting the future. Thus we speak of, for instance, weather prophets. Find Mark 14:65, and determine the meaning of prophet there.

2. In coming to grips with Mark's apocalyptic, I have been greatly helped, and am using material from Eugenio Corsini, *The Apocalypse: The Perennial Revelation of Jesus Christ*, trans. Francis Moloney, Good News Studies (Wilmington, Del.: Michael Glazier, 1983), 50–59. Readers will find a fuller treatment there. Corsini is by no means alone in identifying the crucifixion as the coming of the Son of Man in power and glory. Ched Myers argues similarly in *Binding the Strong Man: A Political Reading of Mark's Story of Jesus* (Maryknoll, N.Y.: Orbis Books, 1988), 324–53.

3. Some hold that Mark also believed that the end of the world was near. This is very unlikely. If you believed the world was about to end, would you put yourself through the agony of writing a Gospel? Would not a placard, suitably worded and worn front and back, be more apt for conveying your message?

4. Francis J. Moloney, S.D.B., brought this chiasm to my notice. Recognition of it greatly simplifies chapter 13.

5. The other Synoptic Gospels, John, and also the canonical ending that was added to Mark's Gospel, show Jesus commissioning the Twelve to preach the Good News. All except John state explicitly that the gospel is to be preached to the whole world. Because Mark chose to end his Gospel at a point of failure on Easter morning, he cannot have the commissioning episode. Instead, Mark is able to announce it implicitly here. Having mentioned it at this point, he will also be able to mention it in the episode of the anointing at Bethany.

6. I have several times questioned interpretations that were too ingenious. However the apocalyptic literary genre, because of its very nature as symbolic code language, requires some ingenuity of the interpreter.

7. Deuteronomy 13:1–2—"If a prophet or one who divines dreams appears among you and promises you a sign or a wonder, and the promised sign or the wonder takes place, and then He says, 'Let us follow other gods' (whom you have not known) 'and let us serve them'"—had warned that false prophets might be able to produce signs and wonders. Some, quite mistakenly, have read this passage as a condemnation of any-

one who produces signs and portents. Several Old Testament passages refute this. Suffice it to mention Dn 3:99–100 (4:2–3 in the Hebrew Bible): "The signs and wonders that the Most High God has favored me with I will gladly make known. How great are his signs, how mighty are his wonders and great are his signs! His kingdom is an everlasting kingdom, and his empire endures for age upon age"; and Dn 6:27: "God saves and sets free, he works signs and wonders in heaven and on earth; he has saved Daniel from the power of the lions."

Note that the church accepts as part of the Old Testament some parts of Daniel that are found in the Septuagint (the early Greek translation), though not found in the Hebrew. Protestants refer to such passages, and to some complete books of the Old Testament (e.g., 1 and 2 Maccabees, the book of Wisdom, Sirach), which were written in Greek, as Apocrypha. Among Catholics they are called Deuterocanonical, which means the supplementary list.

8. John Calvin, one of the leaders of the Reformation, in defending God's sovereignty, was led into teaching that God creates some for heaven and some for hell. We humans have then not one destiny but two alternative destinies. Those who go to hell do so because God created them for that destiny. In defending God's sovereignty, Calvin denied both God's justice and human free will. Calvin would not, I presume, have accepted that his teaching led to this extreme.

9. "The powers in the heavens"—the forces that hold the universe together. They were deemed to be unshakable. Remember that it is picture language. Today Mark might write, "The sun's rising will no longer be certain; and the seas will turn into dust."

10. Mark seems to use "these" and "those" to refer to two different sets of events. The first set, including the destruction of the Temple, is near at hand. The second set of events, as in "that day or that hour," is in the more distant future. "This" and "that" in Greek (and in Latin) can be used to distinguish events that are near (this) and far (that) in time, whether in the past or in the future. However, Mark's usage is not wholly consistent.

CHAPTER 9

MARK 15:1–16:8
JESUS' PASSION AND
RESURRECTION

The purpose of a commentary is not to add to the Gospel but to help the reader hear what the author is saying. Particularly in Mark's passion account there is powerful narrative. For all the reasons given in the early chapters, commentary is necessary. We do need help to see, to hear. But commentary can also interfere. As much as seemed feasible, in this chapter I have transferred comments that are extraneous to the account to the endnotes, so that you the reader can be captured by Mark's bare account, feeling its power. I suggest, then, that you first read the chapter to the end, and only later refer to endnotes.

About a hundred years ago, a scholar named Martin Kähler described Mark as a passion narrative with a long introduction.[1] His description, though inadequate, is true enough to have stuck. The whole story is leading to the moment of recognizing God in Jesus crucified. The listener is reminded of Jesus' fate before his ministry begins, when John the Baptist is handed over. Despite popular enthusiasm for Jesus, early in his ministry an unholy alliance already plots to kill him. Unless Jesus were to become unfaithful to the word God had entrusted to him, the outcome was inevitable. Jesus, the servant of God and of us will now enter upon his final act of service: he will give his life as a ransom for many. God's reign, that Jesus was unable to establish through his powerful works or his preaching, he now trusts God to establish through Jesus' own submitting to death at the hands of evil people. He will approach his passion, feeling the full weight of its meaningless waste, yet trusting God that it is full of purpose.

Although the Gospel reaches its climax in his death on Calvary, the decisive moment in Jesus' passion is not on the cross but in Gethsemane. There Jesus is put to the test. There, depending on God though his prayer seems unanswered, Jesus finds resolve. From that point on, the story traces his becoming more and more abandoned, until he feels abandoned even by God. He dies; and then things begin to change.

The Conspiracy against Jesus: Plotting, Treachery

$^{14:1}$It was two days before the Passover and the festival of Unleavened Bread.^{2} The chief priests and the scribes were looking for a way to arrest Jesus by stealth and kill him;^{3} ^{2}for they said, **"Not during the festival, or there may be a riot among the people."**

In fact, as Mark's audience knows, Jesus' death did take place during the feast. The plotters think that they are in charge of events, but God is.

The Anointing at Bethany: Extravagant Generosity Contrasted with Small-mindedness

^{3}While he was at Bethany in the house of Simon the leper, as he sat at the table, a woman came with an alabaster jar of very costly ointment of nard, and she broke open the jar and poured the ointment on his head.^{4} ^{4}But **some were there who said to one another** in anger, "Why was the ointment wasted in this way? ^{5}For this ointment could have been sold for more than three hundred denarii, and the money given to the poor." And they scolded her. ^{6}But Jesus said, "Let her alone; why do you trouble her? She has performed a good service for me. ^{7}**For you always have the poor**

with you, and you can show kindness to them whenever you wish; but you will not always have me.[5] [8]She has done what she could; **she has anointed my body beforehand for its burial.** [9]Truly I tell you, **wherever the good news is proclaimed** in the whole world, what she has done will be told **in remembrance of her.**"

Mark contrasts generosity with meanness. Surprisingly, the evangelist who most highlights the failure of the apostles, here and in some other places in his account of the passion, refrains from doing so. Those who criticize the woman are simply "some who were there."

The woman is another of the outsiders to the story who yet see. She anoints Jesus' body for its burial; and, though she does not know it, she is giving the burial anointing to the Lord of the Sabbath who, because of the Sabbath, will be buried in haste.[6] She anoints his head, as one would anoint a person for the office of kingship. She sees deeply into events. The Gospel that Jesus speaks of at this point is the account of his passion.

Judas Offers to Betray Jesus:
Betrayal, Treachery

[10]Then Judas Iscariot, **who was one of the Twelve,** went to the chief priests in order **to betray him** to them. [11]When they heard it, they were greatly pleased, and promised to give him money. So he began to look for an opportunity to betray him.

Mark's audience knows that Judas Iscariot was one of the Twelve. Mark listed the Twelve in chapter 3 and underlined then that Judas would betray Jesus. Mentioning it again now serves to highlight the extent of the alienation Jesus is now experiencing. Notice that Mark does not attribute any motive to Judas. Mark, who is often given to earthy and violent language, treats Judas rather gently. The priests' offer of money is mentioned, though, to make the contrast: an unknown woman wastes money on Jesus; one of the Twelve wastes Jesus for money.

The word translated as "betray" is *paradidōmi*. It was used about John the Baptist in chapter 1. Several times Mark uses it in the passive; in which case it is the "divine passive." Jesus is handed over *by God*; however, this must be understood properly. In the Semite's way of thinking, it expresses that God is in charge, and it happened because God, in his providence, allowed it to happen.

Preparations for the Passover: Jesus Is in Charge, Not the Chief Priests

[12]On the first day of Unleavened Bread, when the Passover lamb is sacrificed, his disciples said to him, "Where do you want us to go and make the preparations for you to eat the Passover?"[7] [13]So he sent two of his disciples, saying to them, "Go into the city, and **a man carrying a jar of water** will meet you; follow him, [14]and wherever he enters, say to the owner of the house, '**The Teacher** asks, Where is my guest room where I may eat the Passover with my disciples?' [15]He will show you a large room upstairs, furnished and ready. Make preparations for us there." [16]So the disciples set out and went to the city, and found everything as he had told them; and they prepared the Passover meal.

Carrying water was women's work. A man carrying a pitcher of water would stand out. Before, the chief priests thought that they were managing affairs. Here the disciples think that they are in charge—but Jesus is. The similarity between 14:13 and 11:2 is obvious. As in that verse, Mark is emphasizing that Jesus is in charge of things. He is going to his death of his own free will. Both passages suggest supernatural knowledge on Jesus' part. While such knowledge certainly could have been given to Jesus, this is an understanding of Jesus that Mark generally eschews. On both occasions, Mark has to deal with a narrative problem. Jesus has never been to Jerusalem before—how then can he have supporters there who seem known to him quite personally?

Jesus here calls himself "the Teacher." His most profound teaching will be his own crucifixion.

THE LAST SUPPER

Betrayal, Treachery
(Frame or Inclusion)

[17]When it was **evening**, he came with the Twelve. [18]And when they had taken their places and were eating, Jesus said, "Truly I tell you, one of you will betray me, one who is eating with me." [19]They began to be distressed and to say to him one after another, "Surely, not I?" [20]He said to them, "It is one of the Twelve, **one who is dipping bread into the bowl with me.** [21]For the Son of Man goes as it is written of him, but woe to that one by whom the Son of Man is betrayed![8] It would have been **better for that one not to have been born.**"

Mark mentions evening here and in 15:47. He is relating Jesus' death to Passover. Once again, Mark deals gently with Judas, yet the depth of the betrayal is highlighted by "one who dips bread into the bowl with me." There is no *need* for Mark to mention again the betrayal. The audience has but recently been reminded of it. Mark repeats it here so that Jesus' utter giving of himself (the Eucharist) will be framed by betrayal and desertion, the failure of each of the Twelve. Mark's community in Rome will then be hard put to justify any insistence that those who had failed in the persecution must be forever cast out. Some people, wishing to have certainty that hell has a human population of at least one, have taken "better for that one not to have been born" as a proof that Judas is in hell. If Mark, and Jesus before him, spoke always in the discourse of pure logic, then proof it *would* be. But they were Semites, and Jesus is simply uttering a warning appeal to Judas. My own mother was a Palestinian, born in Jerusalem, and more than once she threatened me, "I will make you wish you had never been born."[9] Sometimes, for variety, she would threaten, "I will kick you from here to Hong Kong."

Utter Generosity
Jesus Pours Out Himself

[22]While they were eating, he took a loaf of bread, and after blessing it he broke it, gave it to them, and said, "Take; this is my body." [23]Then he took a cup, and after giving thanks he gave it to them, **and all of them drank from it.** [24]He said to them, **"This is my blood of the covenant,** which is poured out **for many.** [25]Truly I tell you, I will never again drink of the fruit of the vine until that day **when I drink it new in the kingdom of God."** [26]When they had sung the hymn, they went out to the Mount of Olives.

To the Jew, who would not eat meat with blood in it, "This is my blood" was shocking, horrible; and that guarantees that we are hearing the authentic voice of Jesus. He has linked his approaching death to the Passover sacrifice; and now he links it to the covenant sacrifice. The covenant at Sinai, the old covenant, had been sealed in the blood of sacrifice. There the sacrificial blood was sprinkled on the altar, on the books containing the covenant, and on the people. Jesus goes to his death trusting his Father that his death will be full of meaning and that his life has not been meaningless either. In his blood *the* covenant is sealed.

At 10:38, Jesus had asked James and John, "Can you drink the cup that I must drink?" They had answered, "We can." Mark pointedly notes that *all* drank from the cup. There is no doubt that the cup is Jesus' coming passion. They all drink now at table. When it comes to following him to death though, all will flee from his cup.

Jesus' blood is poured out for many. Here, as in 10:43 ("to give his life as a ransom for many"), there is a clear allusion to Is 53:11, the fourth of the Servant Songs. In his blood will be the ransom of all ("many" here certainly means all, everyone).

"When I drink it new, in the kingdom of God"—Jesus trusts

God that, through his death, the kingdom will be established.
Mark does not supply us with a theology of redemption. He is
writing narrative, not dissertation. But for Mark quite clearly
Jesus' death both reveals and redeems; and, eating and drinking,
we commit ourselves with him.

Betrayal, Desertion
(Frame or Inclusion)

[27]And Jesus said to them, "You will all become deserters; for it is
written, 'I will strike the shepherd, and the sheep will be scattered.'[10] [28]But after I am raised up, I **will go before you to
Galilee.**" [29]Peter said to him, "Even though **all** become deserters, I
will not." [30]Jesus said to him, "Truly I tell you, this day, this very
night, before the cock crows twice, you will deny me three times."
[31]But he said vehemently, "Even though I must die with you, I will
not deny you." And all of them said the same.

Jesus, in the very knowledge that his own will desert him,
promises that he will not desert them. We will hear again, in the
empty tomb, the promise repeated: "He is going before you into
Galilee." Peter self-confidently places himself in a superior position to the others. He *will* stay with Jesus longer than the others,
but his denial of his master will be all the more definite.

Jesus Stays Awake, Pleading
The Disciples Sleep

[32]They went to a place called Gethsemane; and he said to his disciples, "Sit here while I pray." [33]He took with him **Peter and James
and John, and began to be distressed and agitated.**[11] [34]And said
to them, "I am **deeply grieved**, even to death; remain here, and
keep awake." [35]And going a little farther, he threw himself on the
ground and prayed that, if it were possible, the hour might pass
from him. [36]He said, "**Abba**, Father, for you all things are possible;

remove this cup from me; yet, not what I want, but what you want." ³⁷He came and found them sleeping; and he said to Peter, "Simon, are you asleep? Could you not keep awake one hour? ³⁸Keep awake and pray that you may not come into the time of trial; the spirit indeed is willing, but the flesh is weak." ³⁹And again he went away and prayed, saying the same words. ⁴⁰And once more he came and found them sleeping, for their eyes were very heavy; and they did not know what to say to him. ⁴¹He came a third time and said to them, "Are you still sleeping and taking your rest? Enough! **The hour** has come; the Son of Man is betrayed into the hands of sinners. ⁴²Get up, let us be going. See, my betrayer is at hand."

Jesus, faced with the cup he must drink, goes to pieces. The Greek words in v. 33 translated as "distressed and agitated" are very strong words. In *A Grammatical Analysis of the Greek New Testament,* M. Zerwick and M. Grosvenor translate: "he was exceptionally and utterly dismayed," and "he was seized by horror and distress." Jerome Murphy-O'Connor, O.P., has pointed out that Jesus, as he went down from the city into the Kedron Valley, passed by a cemetery. It is still there. It is relatively easy for us to be resigned to death when we think that it is twenty years away from us. Back in chapter 8, Jesus felt tension about facing his destiny. Why else did he call Peter "you Satan." Now his death, a painful death and a shameful death, is imminent; and Jesus is all turmoil within. Murphy-O'Connor has also pointed out that, in Gethsemane, Jesus could easily have gotten up, climbed the few hundred yards to the top of the Mount of Olives, gone down the eastern slope into the desert of Judea, and no available army would have found him there, much less have captured him. Whether these precise thoughts took hold of Jesus' mind, we cannot be certain. Mark's forceful words present a human being without any semblance of "stiff upper lip" or stoic impassiveness in the face of death. He had challenged James and John, "Can you drink the cup that I must drink?" Brashly they said "We can." Faced with that cup, Jesus himself wants to flee it. His proverb-sounding statement to the three, "The spirit is willing, but the flesh is weak" is (at least in this context) an anguished cry from his feeling his own weakness, and his being torn two ways.

He takes Peter and James and John with him, as he had taken those three to witness the theophany, the Transfiguration. As James and John confidently asserted "We can," Peter had asserted, "Even though I must die with you, I will not deny you." Jesus does not hide his brokenness from them, nor his need, "I am deeply grieved, even to death; remain here, and keep awake." Jesus, the Son of God, fully God and fully man, prays to his Father, pleading with that most intimate of words "Abba."[12] In the temptations in the wilderness before his ministry began, angels looked after him. Here he is left alone, his prayer unheard. Yet at the end of three hours he stands, together again, in charge and resolute. The three he bade watch with him are strong; *they* do not need the strength from God that Jesus has sought. Though needed by Jesus, now they sleep.

The Arrest: Betrayal, Desertion

[43]Immediately, while he was still speaking, Judas, one of the Twelve, arrived; and with him there was a crowd with swords and clubs, from the chief priests, the scribes, and the elders.[13] [44]Now the betrayer had given them a sign, saying, "The one I will kiss is the man; (arrest) *seize* him and lead him away under guard." [45]So when he came, he went up to him at once and said, "**Rabbi!**" and **kissed him.** [46]Then they laid hands on him and (arrested) *seized* him. [47]But **one of those who stood near** drew his sword and struck the slave of the high priest, cutting off his ear. [48]Then Jesus said to them, "Have you come out with swords and clubs to arrest me as though I were a bandit? [49]Day after day I was with you in the temple teaching, and you did not (arrest) *seize* me. But let the Scriptures be fulfilled." [50]**All of them deserted him and fled.**

The treachery of Judas is emphasized in the way he greets Jesus. "Rabbi," my master—he calls Jesus, and kisses him.[14]

As in the anointing at Bethany, so here, Mark does not name

the one who struck the high priest's slave. He does not even say that he was a disciple, though, clearly, he must have been. Any notion abroad in Rome that Jesus was a violent bandit, crucified by Pontius Pilate as a fitting outcome for a life of violence, is strongly disowned by Mark.

At the end of the Apocalyptic Discourse, Jesus had bidden the apostles, "Stay awake. If the Son of Man comes unexpectedly, he must not find you asleep." They most certainly did not expect the coming of the Son of Man to be like this—a prisoner, seized and bound. They had gone to sleep, and now all of them desert him and flee. "When the going gets tough, the tough get going." The failure of discipleship is complete. These self-made men are undone. It is their end, and because of the One they had followed, it will be their beginning.

Desertion

[51]A certain young man [*neaniskos*] was following him, wearing nothing but (a linen cloth) *shroud*.[15] They (caught hold of) *seized* him, [52]but he left the linen cloth and ran off naked.

It used to be said that the young man here was Mark. To say that is to miss the depth of meaning in this short aside. I have inserted into the text the Greek word for young man because it will occur again, toward the end of the narrative. There will be a *neaniskos* inside the empty tomb. The young man is linked to Jesus by Mark's recurring use of "seize." He is a disciple. Mark notes that he "was following" Jesus. His clothing is light. The Greek word is *sindōn*, which could mean a thin nightshirt, worn when the nights are warm, an equivalent of cotton pajamas. Mark hardly intends to paint a picture of a warm spring night on the Mount of Olives. The word *sindōn* can also mean a burial shroud, and Mark's symbolic language in this cameo demands that meaning. The young man follows Jesus. He is prepared to die with him; he is already dressed to be buried. As Jesus had been seized, so now the *neaniskos* is seized. But, at the decisive moment, he loses heart. He runs away, leaving the shroud with his captors and himself naked. Clothing expresses the person; at least most cultures think of clothing as expressing the person. To be naked is shame. Confronted with ultimate discipleship, he flees; and he has left to him nothing, nothing but his shame.

JESUS BEFORE THE SANHEDRIN

SANDWICH

Story 1: Peter Follows . . . at a Distance

[53]They took Jesus to the high priest; and all **the chief priests, the elders, and the scribes** were assembled.[16] [54]Peter had **followed him at a distance**, right into the courtyard of the high priest; and he was sitting with the guards, warming himself at the fire.

Mark has just told his audience that all Jesus' disciples had deserted him. He now makes an exception. Peter follows still; that is, he is still a disciple, but at a distance. The bond of discipleship, faced with these developments for which Jesus' had, as best he could, prepared Peter, is becoming tenuous.

Story 2: Jesus Bears Witness Faithfully

[55]Now the chief priests and the whole council were looking for testimony against Jesus to put him to death; but they found none. [56]For many gave false testimony against him, and their testimony did not agree.[17] [57]Some stood up and gave false testimony against him, saying, [58]"We heard him say, 'I will destroy this temple that is made with hands, and in three days I will build another, not made with hands.'" [59]But even on this point their testimony did not agree. [60]Then the high priest stood up before them and asked Jesus, "Have you no answer? What is it that they testify against you?" [61]But he was silent and did not answer. Again the high priest

asked him, **"Are you the Messiah, the Son of the Blessed One?"**[18]
[62]Jesus said, **"I AM; and 'you will see the Son of Man seated at
the right hand of the Power,' and 'coming with the clouds of
heaven.'"** [63]Then the high priest tore his clothes and said, "Why do
we still need witnesses? [64]**You have heard his blasphemy!** What is
your decision?" All of them condemned him as deserving death.

Jesus had uttered no threat against the Temple; in parabolic
action he closed it down. He had, but in private, said that it would
be destroyed, but he had not named himself as the destroyer.[19]
Mark knows perfectly well what he has previously written. If he
records here lying evidence against Jesus, the evidence, nevertheless, is near the truth.[20] Mark is speaking not so much to the
Sanhedrin as to his audience, further developing his Temple theology. The building will be destroyed, he tells his Jewish-
Christians, but it is already redundant. The Temple of God is Jesus
risen from the dead.[21] Jesus, by his death did destroy the Temple,
tore it in two. It has served its purpose. It is now superfluous.
God's glory is hidden no more; and, in his resurrection three days
after, Jesus *has* built a new Temple.

Except for the avoidance of a direct reference to God (the high
priest says "the Blessed One"), the question he has put to Jesus is
taken directly from the title of the book. The high priest *almost*
has it right; but he does not believe, and has Jesus all wrong.
There is no hint of evasion in Jesus' answer; as earlier, in the
Temple, he had evaded baited questions. He answers "I AM." In
view of the likely meaning proposed for "I AM" (6:50) in the context of the exodus events of chapter 6, the "I AM" here is quite
possibly an assertion of divinity, too; and that is the blasphemy
that causes the high priest to tear his clothes.[22] Jesus accepts both
titles put to him by the high priest, and adds the title Son of Man
from the book of Daniel, "you will see the Son of Man seated at
the right hand of the Power" and "coming with the clouds of
heaven."[23] Without *Son of Man*, neither *Christ* nor *Son of God* can
be understood properly. Coming on the clouds of heaven—to sit
in judgment. Jesus claims for himself a divine prerogative. That
too is blasphemy. Fully aware of what he is saying, of the conse-

quence of making such claims in this assembly, and of his utter powerlessness to protect himself from their purposes, Jesus witnesses to the truth. Hanging on the cross he will be the Son of Man and Christ and King and Son of God.

. . . Mockery

[65]Some began to spit on him, to blindfold him, and to strike him, saying to him, "Prophesy!"[24] The guards also took him over and beat him.

As the narrative develops from here, Jesus' kingship will be mentioned repeatedly, and, in place of homage, he will receive mockery. Here, though, he is mocked as a prophet. There is great irony in this. In the hearing before the Sanhedrin, the allegation had been made that he prophesied the end of the Temple. Before the day is out, the Temple will have given place to a new presence of God. Likewise, the crime for which he is condemned, calling himself the Son of God, will be vindicated.

Story 1 Completed: Peter, on Oath, Denies Jesus

[66]While Peter was below in the courtyard, one of the servant-girls of the high priest came by. [67]When she saw Peter warming himself, she stared at him and said, "You also were **with** Jesus, the man from Nazareth." [68]But he denied it, saying, **"I do not know or understand what you are talking about."** And he went out into the forecourt. Then the cock crowed. [69]And the servant-girl, on seeing him, began again to say to the bystanders, "This man is one of them." [70]**But again he denied it**. Then after a little while the bystanders again said to Peter, "Certainly you are one of them; for you are a Galilean." [71]But **he began to curse, and he swore an oath, "I do not know this man you are talking about."** [72]At that moment the cock crowed for the second time. Then Peter remembered that Jesus had said to him, "Before the cock crows twice, you will deny me three times." **And he broke down and wept.**

Peter was one of the Twelve, chosen by Jesus (3:14) to be with him. Peter now denies that he ever was with Jesus.

He had declared his readiness to die with Jesus; but now he goes to pieces. He calls God to witness a lie, and he curses Jesus. The Greek verb is not intransitive. It requires an object. Since the object is not stated, it must be divined from the context. That he is cursing Jesus is the only possibility. Numbering Peter among its leaders was the proud boast of Mark's church in Rome. If Mark highlights Peter's failure, in part this is presumably because Peter had talked of his failure too. There is a need to highlight it now. During the persecution, other members of Rome's church had shown the same weakness that Peter once showed. If any of the more brave Christians of Rome were wanting to excommunicate them forever, then what about Peter?[25] Peter had once called Jesus the Christ. Now he denies even knowing "the man you speak of." There is heavy irony here. In a sense it is true: Peter does not know Jesus. It will not always be that way, though, for Peter has broken down and wept.

THE TRIAL BEFORE PILATE

King of the Jews

[15:1]As soon as it was morning, the chief priests held a consultation with the elders and scribes and the whole council. They bound Jesus, led him away, and handed him over to Pilate. [2]Pilate asked him, "Are you **the King of the Jews?**" He answered him, "**You say so.**"[26] [3]Then the chief priests accused him of many things. [4]Pilate asked him again, "Have you no answer? See how many charges they bring against you." [5]But Jesus made no further reply, so that Pilate was **amazed.** [6]Now at the festival he used to release a prisoner for them, anyone for whom they asked. [7]Now a man called Barabbas was in prison with the rebels who had committed murder during the insurrection.[27] [8]So the crowd came and began to ask Pilate to do for them according to his custom. [9]Then he answered them, "Do you want me to release for you **the King of**

the Jews?" [10]For he realized that it was **out of jealousy** that the chief priests had handed him over.

Pilate will not understand, nor care greatly, about the blasphemy that has justified the Sanhedrin in its decision to hand Jesus over to the Roman authority and to ask for the penalty that is both extreme and terrible. Crucifixion was used by the Romans to provide exemplary punishment for sedition, the crime with which they charge Jesus before Pilate. Mark makes heavy irony of the charge "King of the Jews." Jesus steadfastly shunned the title Messiah because it had become a politically distorted title. Nothing could be further from him than what they meant by "King of the Jews." Questioned by Pilate, Jesus sends the charge back to him. It is true, but not in any way that Pilate, or the leaders among the Jews, or the crowd would understand; and yet it is on the cross that his kingship will be revealed, just as it is on the cross that the Son of Man comes in the glory of his Father. Jesus, king of the Jews, will be mocked repeatedly from now until he dies. There are many references to royalty in chapter 15. Six times Jesus is called king. Jesus endures it all in silence, a silence of such a nature that Pilate feels religious awe, as once Herod Antipas had been perplexed by John the Baptist.

Pilate knows that there is more to it all than Jesus' accusers have told him. Mark notes that Pilate knew it was out of envy that they had handed Jesus over.[28]

Desertion: The Crowd Desert and Deny Jesus

[11]But the chief priests stirred up **the crowd** to have him release Barabbas for them instead. [12]Pilate spoke to them again, "Then what do you wish me to do with the man you call **the King of the Jews?"** [13]They shouted back, "Crucify him!" [14]Pilate asked them, "Why, what evil has he done?" But they shouted all the more, "Crucify him!" [15]So Pilate, wishing to satisfy the crowd, released Barabbas for them; and **after flogging Jesus**, he handed him over to be crucified.[29]

Throughout the story the crowd, not only in Galilee but also here in Jerusalem, have been on Jesus' side. Now, at the last, even they disown him, joining in calling for him to be crucified. Jesus cannot be much more alone than this.

Mockery: King of the Jews

[16]Then the soldiers led him into the courtyard of the palace (that is, the governor's headquarters); and they called together the whole cohort. [17]And **they clothed him in a purple cloak**; and after twisting some thorns into **a crown, they put it on him.**[30] [18]And **they began saluting him, "Hail, King of the Jews!"** [19]**They struck his head with a reed, spat upon him,** and **knelt down in homage to him.** [20]After mocking him, they stripped him of the purple cloak and put his own clothes on him. Then they led him out to crucify him.

An Outsider, Simon, Becomes a Disciple

[21]They compelled a passer-by, who was coming in from the country, to carry his cross; it was Simon of Cyrene, the father of Alexander and Rufus.

Bereft now of all disciples, there is one who, albeit unwillingly, carries the cross. Later, Simon will become a willing follower of the crucified.[31]

Jesus Is Crucified: King of the Jews

[22]Then they brought Jesus to the place called Golgotha (which means the place of a skull). [23]And they offered him **wine mixed with myrrh**; but he did not take it. [24]And they crucified him, and divided his clothes among them, **casting lots** to decide what each

should take.[32] [25]It was nine o'clock in the morning when they crucified him. [26]The inscription of the charge against him read, "**THE KING OF THE JEWS.**"

There is no emphasis at all on Jesus' physical suffering except that he refuses the wine and myrrh, which might have lessened the pain. The guards were entitled to spoils, but his garments are precious little. It was customary for the authorities to fix to the cross a notice of the crime that had brought this awful sentence. The bare title "King of the Jews" invites mockery from all who pass by.

Mockery: Seats on His Right and on His Left in Glory

[27]And with him they crucified two bandits, **one on his right and one on his left.** [29]Those who passed by (derided) *blasphemed* him, shaking their heads and saying, "Aha! You who would destroy the temple and build it in three days, [30]**save yourself,** and come down from the cross!" [31]In the same way the chief priests, along with the scribes, were also mocking him among themselves and saying, "He saved others; he cannot save himself. [32]Let the Messiah, **the King of Israel,** come down from the cross now, so that **we may see and believe.**" Those who were crucified with him also taunted him.

The audience who much earlier had heard about places on Jesus' right and on his left in his glory now finds the two criminals placed, one on his right and the other on his left. Here is Jesus in his glory. Here is the Son of Man coming in the glory of his Father.

The Sanhedrin had found Jesus guilty of blasphemy. Mark here calls the passersby blasphemers. The insults they hurl at Jesus are calling good evil and evil good; and Jesus had called that blasphemy against the Holy Spirit (3:29). Their invitation to Jesus, "save yourself," is likewise made in ignorance of the one who had said, "he who saves his life will lose it." And, in greater ignorance still, by repeating the charge that he would destroy the Temple and in three days rebuild it, they are speaking the meaning of his death—and of the resurrection that will follow. In his glory he is mocked by everybody, passersby, chief priests, scribes, even by the ones on his right and on his left.

Earlier in the Gospel (8:11) the Pharisees sought for a sign. Now chief priests and scribes name the sign they demand. If he comes down, they will *see* and *believe*. One who stands there *will* see and believe, but not through the kind of sign they jeeringly demanded.

Jesus Feels That Even God
Has Deserted Him

³³When it was noon, **darkness came over the whole land** until three in the afternoon. ³⁴At three o'clock Jesus cried out with a loud voice, "Eloi, Eloi, lama sabachthani?" which means, "**My God, my God, why have you forsaken me?**" ³⁵When some of the bystanders heard it, they said, "Listen, he is calling for Elijah." ³⁶And someone ran, filled a sponge with sour wine, put it on a stick, and gave it to him to drink, saying, "Wait, let us see whether Elijah will come to take him down."³³

In the Apocalyptic Discourse, Jesus had spoken of the sun losing its brightness as the Son of Man comes with great power and glory. The darkness comes now. Though it can be explained physically and absurdly as the sirocco, the Khamsin, a dust storm, Mark means the darkness of the end (Am 8:9).

In the garden Jesus had prayed "Abba." Now, deserted by all, Jesus feels that even his Father has departed from him, and he prays, not "Abba" but "Eloi": My God, my God, why have you deserted Me? Again it can be pointed out that the phrase is the beginning of Psalm 22; but it belittles Mark to suggest that he has this cry here merely as a shorthand for the whole of that Psalm. If Mark gives here Jesus' cry of despair, it is to tell his community in Rome that the Son of God too, in the face of cruel death, felt God to be gone.

Faced with this cry of Jesus, some there fumble, as Peter in the earlier theophany (the Transfiguration) had fumbled.

THE CLIMAX OF THE GOSPEL: GOD IS REVEALED

³⁷THEN JESUS GAVE A LOUD CRY AND BREATHED HIS LAST.

No brave last words, no serene majesty, a cry, but not of victory, just a loud scream; and a death as meaningless as the death of any of his followers at the hands of mad Nero.

³⁸AND THE CURTAIN OF THE TEMPLE WAS TORN IN TWO, FROM TOP TO BOTTOM.

The Temple that was the meeting place between God and his people, but also the barrier between God and his people, is destroyed. The innermost part of the Temple in Jerusalem was called the Holy of Holies.[34] Entrance into the Temple was graduated. All including Gentiles and Samaritans could enter the outer court. Into the next court, only Jews, male or female, were permitted. Jewish women were excluded from the next court. Then came the altar of sacrifice. Only priests and Levites entered that court. Beyond this was the Holy of Holies, the dwelling place of God's glory, God's presence among his people. The veil that hung before the Holy of Holies had embroidered on it a representation of the cosmos.[35] The world of the human . . . then the cosmos . . . and, beyond the cosmos, God. The veil spoke, "come this far, this near, but no nearer." Only one person ever entered the Holy of Holies. On the Day of Atonement, the high priest entered, sprinkled the blood of sacrifice, invoked God by name, Yahweh, and withdrew. The veil—God near to his people and yet distant. God needed to be distant. God had told Moses "No one can look on me and live to tell of it." Jesus dies . . . and the veil is torn in two from top to bottom. The Temple is not so much destroyed as surpassed. In the man now dead on the cross God stands revealed. All veils are removed; God's glory is seen. The curtain of the Temple was torn in two from top to bottom . . . the distance is gone, the mystery is no more. In Jesus, God's Son, on a cross crucified, we see manifest the glory of God. The curtain . . . where God meets us . . . but also the barrier . . . and the barrier is torn down . . . torn in two from top to bottom.

39NOW WHEN THE CENTURION, WHO STOOD FACING HIM, SAW THAT IN THIS WAY HE BREATHED HIS LAST, HE SAID, "TRULY THIS MAN WAS (GOD'S SON) *THE SON OF GOD!***"36**

And one standing there sees. At last Jesus is recognized for what in truth he is, God's Son, the Beloved. Once again there is a sign, as at the Transfiguration, but the sign is the least supernatural wonder we might ever demand. It is the way Jesus died that gave sight to this seer. A total outsider with no knowledge of Jesus' works of power, nor even of his teaching—not even a Jew, but he recognizes the Son of God.[37]

Here is the heart of Mark's message. If you want to know Jesus, if you would understand life, and understand Love, if you would see true glory, if you would penetrate the mystery of God, then look at the cross—and not just Christ's cross, out there, a long time ago, but the cross borne in your own life too. The community at Rome knew that already. Paul's letter to them spoke of the cross; Peter's letter from them is full of the cross; but they, like us in every age, succumb to the one heresy that endures in every age, the lie that pretends we can know the depths of God apart from Christ's cross.

All Is Not Lost

40There were also **women** looking on **from a distance**; among them were **Mary Magdalene**, and **Mary the mother of James** the younger **and of Joses,** and **Salome.** [41]These used **to follow him** and provided for him when he was in Galilee; and there were many other women who had come up with him to Jerusalem. [42]When evening had come, and since it was the day of Preparation, that is, the day before the Sabbath, [43]**Joseph of Arimathea,** a respected **member of the council,** who was also himself waiting expectantly for the kingdom of God, **went boldly** to Pilate and asked for the (body) *corpse* of Jesus. [44]Then Pilate **wondered** if he were already dead; and summoning the centurion, he asked him whether he had been dead for some time. [45]When he learned from the centurion that he was dead, he granted the body to Joseph. [46]Then Joseph bought a linen cloth, and taking down the body, wrapped it in the linen cloth, and laid it in a tomb that had been hewn out of the rock. He then rolled a stone against the door of the tomb. [47]**Mary Magdalene and Mary the mother of Joses saw where the body was laid.**

The disciples of John the Baptist buried him. Jesus' disciples are nowhere to be found, at least not those who have appeared in the story thus far. But there is a group, disciples who seemed not to count, outsiders until now. The women *followed* him from Galilee, and now they have followed him to Calvary. They are at a distance. The bond of discipleship has weakened, but it is not broken. There is another outsider to the story, a member of the Sanhedrin itself. As Jesus' death brought sight to the centurion, so it brings courage to Joseph. And so Jesus' corpse (Mark uses the much harsher word than body) will receive decent burial, if not from the Twelve, then from these. Pontius Pilate authorizes it. The man who had begun to feel awe in the presence of Jesus, leaves the story feeling awe again that so quickly he died.

Mark notes the names of some of the women. The mother of James (the younger) and of Joses is a relative of Jesus (cf. 6:3), one of those who once thought that he had gone mad.[38]

MARK 16:1–8: HE IS RISEN

[16:1]When the Sabbath was over, Mary Magdalene, and Mary the mother of James, and Salome bought spices, so that they might go

and anoint him. ²And very early **on the first day of the week,
when the sun had risen,** they went to the tomb. ³They had been
saying to one another, "Who will roll away the stone for us from
the entrance to the tomb?" ⁴When they looked up, they saw that
the stone, which was very large, had already been rolled back. ⁵As
they entered the tomb, they saw **a young man** [*neaniskos*], **dressed
in a *brilliant* white robe, sitting on the right side;** and they were
alarmed. ⁶But he said to them, "Do not be alarmed; you are looking for Jesus of Nazareth, who was crucified. **He has been raised;**
he is not here. Look, there is the place they laid him. ⁷But **go, tell
his disciples and Peter that he is going ahead of you to Galilee;
there you will see him,** just as he told you."³⁹

The Sabbath is over, because God is about to begin anew the
work of creation.

"Very early on the first day of the week"—there is a new week,
and the new creation, which will not be complete until Jesus
comes again. God's first work in that new week is to separate light
from darkness, "the sun had risen." The women do not know that
yet, and old cares, stones to be rolled away, occupy their minds.

They reach the tomb, and inside they see the young man.⁴⁰ At
Gethsemane, having abandoned discipleship, he was left with
nothing but nakedness and shame. Now Jesus is risen, and with
no word of rebuke, the *neaniskos* is clothed in discipleship,
clothed more brilliantly than he was ever before. He is not the
only one so restored. He, who once had threatened to disown
those who brought shame on him, simply restores them: "Go and
tell the disciples . . . and Peter." Peter was the last one to deny, but
his denial was the worst.

"He is going before you into Galilee," where, not in the cozy
world of theocratic Jerusalem but in the ambiguous world of
Galilee, the messy world that is not life as we want it but life as it
is, the divine mess—there you will see him. Where he first began
with you . . . now that you are broken . . . he can truly begin. So
the women are to tell them—for they have been appointed the
evangelists of the resurrection.

[8]SO THEY WENT OUT AND FLED FROM THE TOMB, FOR TERROR AND AMAZEMENT HAD SEIZED THEM; AND THEY SAID NOTHING TO ANYONE, FOR THEY WERE AFRAID. . . .

He is risen. Things will be different from now on. God has spoken a final yes to it all, a yes we can never forget. There will be no more worrying, no more care, no more fear, no more darkness . . . and they said not a word to anyone because they were afraid . . . the evangelists fail to evangelize. So ends the beginning, but the Good News lives still.

And Mark leaves his community in Rome, and us, to reflect that the Good News of the resurrection, the news the women were afraid to speak, has reached them. Failure is not the end of their story, nor of ours.

EXCURSUS 5
A NOTE ABOUT CRUCIFIXION

The writings of Jesus' time hardly ever mention crucifixion. The Romans were embarrassed about their using this form of punishment. Crucifixion had been devised originally by the Persians, to please the god Ahura-Mazda. They decided that the bodies of condemned criminals, if allowed to touch the earth, insulted the god.

When Julius Caesar was a young officer, he was in charge of a regiment of soldiers being conveyed by ship to the Middle East. The ship was set upon by pirates, who robbed and plundered. Caesar vowed to them that one day he would capture them and crucify them. As it happened, he did capture them, and began setting stakes into the ground to crucify them all. The pirates begged for mercy. Caesar decided he would be merciful. He would first slit their throats, and then crucify them. On their knees, they praised him for his mercy. The orator Cicero said about crucifixion that it was so barbarous that its name should not even be mentioned among Roman citizens.

The crucified was usually flogged first, barbarous enough in itself. Then he or she had to carry the cross-beam to the place of execution. The uprights were already in place. While some were fixed to the cross by ropes, certainly some were nailed to the cross. There was usually a small cross-beam on which the crucified could half-sit. This prolonged the agony. It could take days for a condemned person to die. The condemned were always crucified in a public place. The purpose of such a cruel death was to keep the population loyal. They were usually crucified stark naked; though it is thought that in Palestine, in deference to Jewish sensibilities, a condemned man was left with his loin cloth, and a condemned woman left appropriately covered. Sometimes the corpses of the crucified were left on the cross to decay and become prey for birds and wild beasts. The penalty of crucifixion was abolished by the emperor Constantine.

The book of Deuteronomy (21:22–23) says "cursed is the man who hangs from a tree." By the time of Jesus, crucifixion was held to come under that curse (the Dead Sea Scrolls provide evidence). Paul had to grapple hard with the fact that the Christ had come under a curse of the law—to be cursed by the law was, surely, to be cursed by God. Quite possibly, the house of Annas had determined to have Jesus crucified for that very reason.

Excursus 6
The Attempted Endings of Mark

Some scholars still maintain that Mark did not end his Gospel at 16:8. Accepting that neither the present canonical ending nor the two other endings extant came from Mark's pen, they regard the true ending as lost. If my approach to Mark sheds little new light on the Gospel of Mark, at least it shows that Mark's ending is in harmony with the body of his narrative.

Below is the canonical appendix. It will easily be seen that it does not even follow logically from v. 8. Its author has drawn on Matthew, Luke, and John.

Mk 16:8. So they went out and fled from the tomb, for terror and amazement had seized them; and they said nothing to anyone, for they were afraid.

Mk 16:9–20. Now after he rose early on the first day of the week, he appeared first to Mary Magdalene, from whom he had cast out seven demons. [10]She went out and told those who had been with him, while they were mourning and weeping. [11]But when they heard that he was alive and had been seen by her, they would not believe it. [12]After this he appeared in another form to two of them, as they were walking into the country. [13]And they went back and told the rest, but they did not believe them. ¹⁴Later he appeared to the eleven themselves as they were sitting at the table; and he **upbraided them for their lack of faith and stubbornness, because they had not believed those who saw him after he had risen.** ¹⁵And he said to them, "Go into all the world and proclaim the good news to the whole creation. ¹⁶The one who believes and is baptized will be saved; but the one who does not believe will be condemned. ¹⁷And these signs will accompany those who believe: by using my name they will cast out demons; they will speak in new tongues; ¹⁸they will pick up snakes in their hands, and if they drink any deadly thing, it will not hurt them; they will lay their hands on the sick, and they will recover." ¹⁹So then the Lord Jesus, after he had spoken to them, was taken up into heaven and sat down at the right hand of God. ²⁰And they went out and proclaimed the good news everywhere, while the Lord worked with them and confirmed the message by the signs that accompanied it.

While v. 19 is beautiful (certifying the happy ending without which God is a cruel joker), as is also v. 16, the appendix as a whole is no tribute to Mark. Superficially, v. 14 might seem Markan, but Jesus' upbraiding of them here has a quite different "feel" from his rebukes in the Gospel. Of the signs that are listed, "picking up snakes" may reflect an episode during Paul's sojourn on the island of Malta. Taken as a whole, they are the opposite of what Mark would regard as revealing God. They are more like the stunts the Markan Jesus rejects. Finally, v. 16 has been the justification of "outside the church, no salvation." The world is neatly divided into "believing and saved," "nonbelieving and condemned." What would Mark, for whom outsiders can be insiders, and insiders outsiders, make of all this? I can imagine Mark, as these verses were penned crying out to the Holy Spirit, "Stop him (or her) before it's too late" and the Holy Spirit replying, as often the Spirit has to, "Leave it be, leave it be! It will come right in the end!"

The following are the other endings, neither of which, thank God, is canonical.

This ending, often printed as an appendix to Mark, is known as the Shorter Ending. It attempts to follow on from v. 8:

But they quickly reported to Peter and the others who were with him everything that they had been told. And afterwards Jesus himself sent out through them, from East to West, the sacred and imperishable proclamation of Eternal Salvation.

A third attempt at ending Mark's Gospel for him is weird and reminds us of those converts who tried to import into the Gospel ideas that were alien, unhealthy. It begins after v. 14 of the canonical ending:

> And they excused themselves saying, "this age of lawlessness and faithlessness is under the power of Satan who, by the work of unclean spirits prevents the truth and power of God from being apprehended; therefore, reveal Your justice now." They were speaking to Christ, and Christ said in reply: "The measure of the years of Satan's power is about to be ended, but other terrible things are drawing near. Yet for the sinners I was delivered up to death, that they might turn to the truth and sin no more and so inherit the spiritual and undying glory of justification which is in heaven."

Mark would have none of this blaming it all on the devil. Among the enemies Jesus has to deal with, the devils are minor. The real enemy of the Gospel is myself, when I choose to harden my heart.

Notes

1. In arithmetical terms, while Mark's Gospel is by far the shortest, his passion is, comparatively, the longest of the three Synoptic accounts, being only forty words shorter than Luke's, four hundred and fifty words shorter than Matthew's. Out of sixteen chapters (665 verses), six chapters (241 verses) are about the last week of Jesus' life.

2. In Jewish calculation, the day itself is counted. Since, according to Mark, Passover was on a Thursday night and the new day began at sunset, "two days before" is Wednesday. The feast of Unleavened Bread was celebrated over a full week, that is, eight days, an octave. It began with Passover. In primordial antiquity, the feast of Unleavened Bread celebrated the barley harvest. Likewise, in the same antiquity, Passover celebrated the dropping of the spring lambs. Originally, then, both were nature feasts and continued to have that aspect. However, since God's delivering his people from Egypt, both had become first and foremost salvation feasts.

Matthew and Luke follow Mark in placing Passover on the Thursday night, the night before Jesus' death. John places the Passover that year on Friday night. Yet the Johannine Last Supper has suggestions of Passover about it. All agree in linking Jesus' last meal and his death with the feast of Passover. His death is the Passover, our deliverance.

The early Christians did not celebrate the Eucharist like a Passover meal. If they connect the Eucharist with Passover, Jesus himself must have made the connection.

3. "By stealth"; see Pss 10:7; 35:20; 52:2.

4. In Luke, there is a divergent account of a woman washing Jesus' feet (Lk 7:36–50). The event takes place in the house of a Simon, but in Galilee. Simon is identified as a Pharisee unfriendly to Jesus; and there is no mention of his being a leper. It is highly unlikely that two different events lie behind the two traditions. It is a rather extreme example of how, in different traditions, the telling of an event can go in quite different directions.

I have never seen an explanation given of why Mark supplies the name of the host. It may simply reflect the tradition.

A denarius was a day's (sustenance) wage for a laborer. The cost of the ointment is nearly a year's wages.

There is, of course, a problem, evidenced several times in Mark's account of Jesus' ministry in Jerusalem. If he has never been there before, how does he know some people there quite well.

5. "The poor you will have always with you" is another much-abused Markan text, used by the wealthy to justify neglecting or even exploiting the poor. This very contextualized statement is treated as though Jesus were uttering an eternal and immutable divine decree. Jesus is alluding to Dt 15:11: "Since there will never cease to be some in need on the earth, I therefore command you, 'Open your hand to the poor and needy neighbor in your land.'"

6. Some read into this that she knows that he will not be dead for long enough to be able to be anointed; that is, she knows he will rise from the dead. This is reading far too much into the evangelist's intention. It could be counterargued that, if she knows that, why bother about anointing him at all? Likewise to read from it that Jesus expected to be buried in a common grave, without any one to anoint his body may be correct; but it is dangerous to go beyond what Mark intends to say. Jesus does not say here that there will be no one to anoint his body after his death.

7. Only a few verses previously Mark has followed the Jewish reckoning for a day. Here, he reverts to the Roman midnight-to-midnight reckoning of a day. Either that or else Mark was not a Jew, and hence was inaccurate about the two feasts (but everyone recognizes that the Gospel has an Aramaic substratum). Mark wants to emphasize the connection between the paschal lamb and Jesus' going to his death.

8. Jesus could find his death prophesied—albeit somewhat veiled as prophecies generally are—in Isaiah's Servant Songs, in Psalms, especially Psalm 22, in the book of Wisdom, and in the fate of the prophets.

9. I have been told often that, in the language in which I describe the way Semites think and talk, I am denigrating them. On the contrary, I see it as a superior gift. We do not define a human by the qualities of mind that make us different from the animal world. The uniqueness of being human is that we are at once mind and matter, not as two separate principles—a dualism—but as one. Those who eschew the kind of thinking that is both spiritual and material are themselves thinking as dualists.

10. Zechariah 13:7: "Strike the shepherd, says the Lord of hosts, that the sheep may be scattered; I will turn my hand against the little ones."

11. Gethsemane means "olive press." Mark does not translate it into Greek. Though this is possibly an oversight, it more likely means that the word has already passed into Christian usage. Neither does he translate "rabbi" (see below, v. 45). The word *rabbi* would have been well known in pagan circles. One in every twelve persons in the Roman Empire was a Jew.

12. This Aramaic word occurs only three times in the New Testament. This is its only occurrence in the Gospels. It is used by Paul twice to describe the way we should see God—Gal 4:6 and Rom 8:15. The two passages are similar. Jesus called God "Abba," and he taught us to so see God as "Abba." Many scholars have argued that the word bears such a totally unexpected degree of intimacy that, if it had not come from Jesus himself, it would not have been part of the kerygma either. However, *Abba* is sometimes described as baby-talk, equivalent to "mumma," "mummy," or "dadda," "daddy." The word was used by adults as well as children. It might be represented better by our "mum," "mom," or "dad." It does not have the formal quality usually associated with the address "mother," "father," or "sir."

13. The audience has certainly no need now to be reminded that Judas is one of the chosen Twelve. Mark, in emphasizing the horror of betrayal by an intimate, is possibly thinking of some of the betrayals during the Neronian persecution. The betrayal of Peter and Paul by fellow Christians would still be felt sorely in the Roman community.

14. Twice Peter calls Jesus Rabbi—at the Transfiguration and when he finds the fig tree withered. As noted earlier, Jesus in this Gospel is called most frequently, by friend and foe, Teacher. Rabbi has more connotations of familiarity than Teacher.

15. The inspiration for this vignette may be Am 2:16: "and those who are stout of heart among the mighty shall flee away naked in that day, says Yahweh." See also Ez 16:1–15, 60, 63.

16. In sum, the Sanhedrin. The chief priests, elders, and scribes have emerged as Jesus' main opposition in Jerusalem. Jesus' opponents within

Galilee were identified as the Pharisees and the Herodians; and in Jerusalem they had set the trap question for Jesus, "Is it lawful to pay tribute to Caesar, or not?" However, the Pharisees and the Herodians do not play any part in the actual condemnation of Jesus. They had little representation in the Sanhedrin, which was dominated by Sadducees. Raymond Brown has pointed out that the Pharisees played a passive role in Jesus' condemnation. If they had sided with Jesus, it would have been much more difficult for the Sanhedrin to have gotten rid of him.

17. The law of Moses required at least two witnesses whose testimony agreed.

18. Scholars have not been able to find in pre-Christian literature any text that identifies the Messiah as "the Son of God." As mentioned at the end of chapter 2, for a period some scholars proposed that "the Son of God" was a Christian way of making Jesus intelligible to the pagans, a way of rendering *theios anēr*, that is, a man with godlike powers. More detailed research has refuted this endeavor to remove the claim that Jesus was divine. The term *theios anēr* was hardly known until about a hundred years after the time of Jesus.

19. To describe the Temple "made by human hands," Mark uses the Greek word *cheiropoiēton*. Whenever this word is used in the Septuagint (the translation of the Old Testament into Greek) it refers to false or idolatrous worship. Mark may intend this meaning. If he does, then only the failure of the witnesses to agree in their perjured evidence prevented the Sanhedrin from convicting Jesus immediately of blasphemy. See Robert J. Daly, S.J., *The Origins of Christian Sacrifice* (Philadelphia: Fortress Press, 1978), 55.

20. And remarkably similar to Jn 2:19.

21. A targum of Zec 6:12 reads: "And you shall say to him, 'Thus says the Lord of Hosts, this man, Messiah is his name. He will be revealed, and will be exalted, and he will build the Temple of the Lord.'" Similarly, a targum of Is 53:5 specifies the Messiah as the builder of the Temple, "he will build the Temple which was profaned because of our transgressions, and delivered up because of our sins." A second-century B.C.E. writing, *1 Enoch* (90:28–29) says that, in the final age, a new Temple will be built.

22. The rending of garments is still used by Jewish men to express deep horror or grief. At the time of Jesus, blasphemy, for which the penalty was death, had become a word used rather loosely. Later its meaning was defined more strictly.

23. While there is no doubt whatsoever that by "the Power" Mark means God, there is also no precedent for so referring to God. Mark does not appear to give this circumlocution any special meaning.

24. Nearly one-third of Mark's passion narrative consists of mockery.

25. Christians who had suffered for the faith in the persecutions, but had not been put to death, were called confessors (accent on the middle syllable).

26. Ralph Martin translates the sense of Jesus' answer as "You do well to ask" (*Mark, Evangelist and Theologian* [Grand Rapids, Mich.: Zondervan, 1973], 178).

27. I read somewhere a long time ago—but have not been able to confirm—that Barabbas was involved in a revolt about a year previously. This revolt had been betrayed to Pilate by the Pharisees. Pilate's ruse *should* have been successful. Both Sadducees and Pharisees would have wanted to see the end of Barabbas.

28. Undoubtedly envy *(phthonos)* was part of the reason, but why has Mark emphasized it? In the letter Clement wrote from Rome to Corinth in 96 C.E., he mentions that Peter and Paul were betrayed through *phthonos*. No doubt Mark's audience both know and feel what the envy within their community had done. I suggest that Mark highlights *phthonos* for that very reason. The book of Wisdom says that envy is the devil's motive for bringing death on our race.

29. Three times in two verses Mark uses Latinisms. One, *praetorion*, is to be expected. To transliterate the Latin *flagellare* ("to flog") into Greek as *phragellein* is unexpected. Least of the three to be expected is Mark's transliteration of the Latin *satisfacere* ("to satisfy"). *Satisfacere* is a compound Latin word—*facere* ("to make") and *satis* ("enough"). Mark having no single Greek word to convey the meaning of *satisfacere,* breaks the word up into its two components and then translates each into Greek. Thus, *hikanon* ("enough") followed by *poiēsai* ("to make"). The presence of such Latinisms argues that Mark, while most at home with Aramaic, felt sometimes more comfortable with Latin than with Greek. In the last case he was undeniably more comfortable with Latin.

30. Roman Soldiers wore a scarlet cape over their armor. Almost certainly it is with one of these capes that they invest and mock Jesus. Mark calls it purple, however, because purple was the imperial color. Mark is asserting for Jesus the highest kingship.

31. Obviously Mark's audience in Rome must have known who Alexander and Rufus were. Most likely, then, Simon of Cyrene became a Christian. Paul in Romans (16:13) mentions "greet Rufus, and his mother, who has been a mother to me." There was, then, a Christian in Rome named Rufus. However, to go from there to arguing that it is Rufus, son of Simon of Cyrene, is tenuous. As a matter of interest, in the cemetery on the way from Jerusalem to the Mount of Olives there is

inscribed on one of the tombs "Simon, the father of Alexander and Rufus."

32. Mark refers to casting lots because it is mentioned in Psalm 22. There are seven references to this Psalm in chapter 15.

33. In Jesus' Galilean dialect, his saying "Eloi" sounded to a southerner like "Elijah." I am indebted to Paul Stenhouse, M.S.C., for pointing this out to me.

34. Having such an innermost part of the Temple was not peculiar to the Jews. It was common in temples of Egypt and the Middle East. In pagan temples, the Holy of Holies housed the statue of the god.

35. The Jewish historian Flavius Josephus described the Temple veil. The validity of Mark's statement does not depend on the veil being as Josephus described it; however, it enhances Mark's interpretation. If Mark's audience did not know about the decoration of the veil before the Holy of Holies, they would miss the nuance of it. Did they know? Probably, his fellow Jewish-Christians did and the Gentiles did not. The Jewish-Christians were the ones who, faced with the imminent destruction of the Temple at the hands of the Romans, needed reassurance.

36. As in the title of the Gospel (1:1), the definite article does not appear before "Son of God." The absence of the definite article does not imply "a" rather than "the" Son of God. This was discussed in dealing with the title of the Gospel. E. C. Colwell has noted that, from the study of Greek usage, when a predicate noun precedes the verb (as is the case in both of these places), the definite article is usually omitted (see Martin, *Mark, Evangelist and Theologian*, 131). Thus, in Mk 3:11, where unclean spirits cry out "you are the son of God," the verb *ei* (are) comes before the predicate, and Mark has the definite article *ho* (the) *huios tou theou* (son of God). But here, when the verb comes last, Mark omits the definite article.

37. Raymond Brown has noted an important parallel between events immediately after Jesus' Baptism (1:10–11) and these events immediately after his death (*The Death of the Messiah* [New York: Doubleday, 1994], 2:1100). After the Baptism, the heavens are torn apart and God proclaims "You are my beloved Son." Here the veil is torn apart and the centurion proclaims "Truly this man was the Son of God." The four events immediately after Jesus' death are in two pairs. The events in the second pair are about discipleship. The events in the first pair are about the revelation of God. All four events are positive. Some scholars see the first event negatively; the rending of the veil is the destruction of the Temple, God answering wrathfully their killing his Son. I cannot imagine that Mark would, immediately after Jesus' death for all, portray God acting

wrathfully, vindictively. And, if God does so act against the Jewish leadership, why does God not act wrathfully also by punishing Jesus' disciples? The rending of the veil is the surpassing of the Temple, destruction if you like, but as something positive, not negative.

38. Mark says nothing about Mary Magdalene or Salome. Presumably, his audience knew of them from the preaching of the Gospel. Likewise, they must know why James is called the Younger—to distinguish him from James the son of Zebedee and brother of John. Their noting where the corpse was laid may serve an apologetic purpose—if some were alleging that the reason they never found Jesus' corpse was that they went to the wrong tomb. This is unlikely, because it would be just someone's word against another. More likely, as with the use of the word "corpse," Mark is asserting the horrible reality: the Son of God is dead.

39. In Jewish law, the witness of women was not acceptable testimony except in domestic matters and other matters pertaining to women.

40. Some regard the young man as an angel. The description of him is a fairly standard Old Testament description of an angel. He *is* an angel. Mark means both. In fact, the young man is more than that. He is at the right hand side—and that is where Jesus is. Mark is able to speak on several levels, but discipleship restored is Mark's primary meaning.

THE FATE OF MARK

A part from a few scholars, mostly of fundamentalist leaning, the world of biblical criticism holds that Mark's Gospel came first.[1] Both Matthew and Luke, in writing their Gospels depended on Mark. Their fundamental debt to him was to have this kind of writing we call Gospel. If Mark had not spoken to Christians through the life of their Master, there is no reason to believe that either Matthew or Luke would have conceived this idea. Luke had Mark before him as he wrote. He had other sources, too. Though he followed Mark's model—and Luke fully exploits the potential of Mark's journey to Jerusalem—he used Mark with freedom. Matthew likewise had Mark before him and followed Mark's Gospel sometimes, I think unsurely.[2] In fact, over 90 percent of Mark's Gospel is found also in Matthew.

The Gospel of John does not fit the definition of Gospel given above at the end of chapter 1. That Gospel is not the author addressing his community in its need. It is the Johannine community sharing with the Christian world at large its vision. Nevertheless, the Fourth Gospel bears enough resemblance to the other three for the Johannine community to have been familiar with at least one of them. While points of contact between John and Matthew, and between John and Luke, have been noted, a number, though not a majority, of scholars think that the Johannine community knew Mark. Some concepts that are important but inchoate in Mark are fully developed in John. Among these concepts, the most noteworthy are glory, kingship, and "I AM." There are a number of important events that are missing from the Fourth Gospel. Among these are the

Transfiguration, the Agony in the Garden, and especially the institution of the Eucharist. Yet each of these events is made up for in John. For example, John chapter 6 contains a very important theology of the Eucharist. It is possible that the reason the events are absent from John is that John's community cherished Mark and did not want to rewrite it. In the fifth century, Augustine proposed that the Fourth Gospel was meant to complete the other three.[3]

The Gospel of Mark, then, had an influence well beyond what its author intended. How, though, did it fare with the community for whom Mark wrote? It may well have failed. When Ambrosiaster said that the Romans received the Gospel with a peculiarly Jewish bent, he was surely not noting something completely in the past.[4] The only document available to us that mirrors the thinking of the leading Christians of Rome at the end of the first century is the letter known as *1 Clement*. Mark's Gospel was written around 70 C.E. *1 Clement* was written fewer than thirty years later in 96 C.E. It is clear that Clement knew and used the Letter to the Hebrews. He did not, however, absorb the message of Hebrews.[5] Hebrews agrees with Mark in saying that the Temple and its ritual have been fulfilled and surpassed in Christ, the Eternal Priest. *1 Clement*, however, lives in a Jewish-Christian world. A cursory reading of it is enough to see that it is poles apart from, and quite inferior to, Mark. The author of *1 Clement* may have known Mark. *1 Clement* quotes from Is 29:3 in precisely the same wording as Mark 7:6.[6] There are in *1 Clement* references to Jesus' teaching that may come from Mark, although they may simply have come from the oral tradition. For example, *1 Clement* makes use of a teaching that the one who humbles himself will be exalted. While this teaching is found in Mark, there is nothing in the teaching itself or in the way Clement phrases the teaching that points compellingly to Mark as its source. The epistle sometimes gives a teaching of Jesus that is not found in Mark. To the reader familiar with Mark, the God of *1 Clement* is far less intimate than the God of the first Gospel; and, if Mark pointed to a future for the church beyond Judaism, the church of *1 Clement* is still Judeo-centric. In reading *1 Clement*, one has to remind oneself that the

Temple in Jerusalem had been destroyed a quarter of a century before the writing of that epistle. In sum, one does not gain the impression that the author of *1 Clement* has been nourished by Mark. If *1 Clement* reflects the thinking of the church in Rome—and most likely that is the case—then Judeo-Christians retained control of the church in Rome. As a corollary, it can be said that the Gospel of Mark was quite possibly rejected by its primary audience. In other words, the Gospel of Failure may well have failed itself.

I have suggested that Matthew did not always understand the message of Mark. The second-century attempts to supply an ending for Mark prove that Mark's purpose was no longer understood. The first writer to name an author for this Gospel damned Mark with faint praise, describing him as having written down Jesus' words and deeds, but "not in any order."

As the living memories of Jesus receded into the past, the agenda changed. Christians wanted "facts about Jesus." In 175 C.E. the writer Tatian produced his *Diatessaron,* the life of Jesus put together by harmonizing the four Gospels. The individuality of each Gospel became blurred. Of the four Gospels Mark suffered most. If facts about Jesus were what mattered, and if Mark is nearly all found in Matthew, and if some of Mark's facts were embarrassing, it was inevitably destined to become the "also-ran" Gospel. Add to this the inelegance of Mark's Greek, and Mark was doomed to neglect. The Gospel of Mark had to wait nearly four hundred years before any author bothered to write a full commentary on it, and a further three hundred years for another commentary. Not until the second millennium did the third full commentary on Mark appear. It had become the Cinderella Gospel.

In the eighteenth century, with the advent of historical criticism, Mark came to be labeled the primitive Gospel, the only Gospel from which a true picture of Jesus of Nazareth could be gleaned. Mark became the darling of the skeptics; however, that search for the historical Jesus was to lead eventually to the realization that Mark is far from being a primitive account of Jesus. Only in this century has the genius of Mark been grasped. Even the compilers of the Roman lectionary, a work undertaken in the 1960s, have not done justice to Mark.

Sometimes I ask people who are scripturally literate which is their favorite Gospel. Most often, with little hesitation, they will say the Gospel of Mark. I hope that readers of this Gospel will treasure the word made indelible by the pen of stump-fingered Mark.

GOSPEL OF FAILURE—GOSPEL OF HOPE?

One might devote several chapters yet to exploring different aspects of Mark. We could study discipleship in Mark, locales (the sea, sea-crossings, synagogues, houses, mountains) in Mark, the Markan Jesus, the Temple in Mark. The aim of this work has been confined to helping the reader feel at home in this first of the Gospels. Readers will grow more readily in their own intimacy with Mark by exploring such themes for themselves. Students with the scripture on computer can explore it quite speedily by utilizing the scripture program's concordance. However, they should also seek that more thoroughgoing familiarity with the text which brings discovery of new treasures and food for the soul. That familiarity can hardly be gained without quietly reading the text.

Mark wrote his Gospel to give hope to a community that had failed, a community that had thought itself strong but then found itself weak. The kind of hope he offered was a sober hope. There is no promise that summer is just around the corner, no illusory guarantee of "living happily ever after." His message is rather that it was a mess in the beginning too, doomed to fail, and yet is living still. The kind of hope that comes from success—"Everybody is looking for you"—is not the hope Mark offers. The kind of confidence that comes from having the world divided quite clearly into two groups only, Catholic and non-Catholic, much the same as some Jews still divide the world into Jew and Goy, that self-confidence Mark firmly rejects. Just as firmly, he rejects any vision of reality that would put the blame for our troubles on forces beyond us, the world of the devil. The enemy of God's reign is human; the Gospel's opponent is me, my heart.

Mark promises that the Gospel will continue. Equally he promises that it will always be a battle. The reign of God is as unrealistic as was Jesus; and, like those he first called, I will know better. Continually, I will find the Gospel too much; and I will build models, look-alikes that fall short, for the cross is left out. Yet when the end comes, God's harvest is sure.

Aged now fifty-nine, I grew up in a church that felt itself strong. The older I grew, the more certain it grew. We were a minority, but a strong and sure minority who could hold our heads high. We had an immediate affinity with any other Catholic anywhere in the world. To be Catholic was more basic than nationality, class, or race. As warrant for our self-confidence, churches were full every Sunday, and fish-and-chip shops were full every Friday. Then along came the Second Vatican Council that said "back to the Gospel"; and then, just as we changed to become true to the world by renewal in the Gospel, the world itself changed. Now we know ourselves weak. The disillusionment we Catholics suffer now is as great as the disillusionment the apostles felt on Good Friday. If, in the 1950s and 1960s, we were really as strong as we thought that we were, we would not now be weak, as weak as we feel. A lot of the strength of the church of Rome in the 1950s and 1960s was as unsurely founded as was that of Rome's church in the fifties and sixties of the first century.

Our only true strength is in living the Gospel. To the extent that we are now more true to the Gospel, the failure we feel is the failure Christ felt. To the extent that we yearn for the glory dreamed of by the Twelve, their failure is ours. Our choice is not one of success or failure. Our choice is to yearn for a success that will fail us, or to live in the failing that will be God's success.

The reign of God, the reign that God's Son could not bring by his preaching, remains still to come. It does come. Our efforts are not doomed to fail eternally; but the day we fool ourselves, saying "we have here the reign of God" we have ourselves moved outside. Always, we will be tempted to settle for something that looks like God's reign. The solid phalanx that was the church I grew up in, the church where I was proud to belong, the church about which I could stick out my chest, was not the realization of the reign of God. Nor were the ages of Christendom, the ages that built the great medieval cathedrals; they were not the reign of God. The Middle Ages had much that was barbarous, much that was truly dark. Indeed, the Wagnerian Operas that resurrected the ancient myths in the founder of Nazism were the revenge of pagan gods on a land where the Gospel, not allowed to be the yeast that works slowly within, had been imposed by decrees.[7] God's reign does come, and often surprises; but the grand vision of a world where truth is *imposed* is a vision not of God's reign, not of hearts tamed, but of hearts chained.

To be truly disciples is too much for us. For Christ, too, at the end, it tore him apart. To his Father, he cried "Let this cup pass." We will not change the world till we take up the cross; and, when it comes to the cross, we flee. Often we flee and are naked. To be true to Christ is too much to ask, and the mess and failure will always be there; yet out of that mess God is shaping his dominion. It is the divine mess.

During World War II, the BBC played the first bar of Beethoven's *Fifth Symphony*. It is, in Morse code, the letter V—V for Victory. That is well remembered by those who lived through the blitz. Not so well remembered are some lines the BBC quoted often to help inspire Britons, so that their darkest hour might become their finest hour. The lines were penned by G. K. Chesterton, part of his epic poem, "The Ballad of the White Horse":

> I tell you nought for your comfort,
> yea, nought for your desire,
> save that the sky grows darker yet
> and the sea rises higher.[8]

They seem hardly words of hope, yet they did inspire hope and endurance. The hope Chesterton speaks of here is the hope Mark offers us. That sort of promise which says, "So you think things are bad? They will be worse yet!" *can* inspire people to endure, to endure *together*.

The triumphant last words of John's Jesus, "It is consummated," surely inspire. The serene last words of Luke's Jesus, "Father, into thy hands I commend my spirit," inspire too. Yet the despairing last words of Mark's Jesus, "My God, why . . . ," most surely bring him closer to us, and us closer to him. That is the kind of hope the Gospel of Failure kindles.

To a community that had failed, Mark says that there was failure in the beginning too, but the gospel is still at work. To us now who, if we are realists, know that the church is in a mess and that it is getting worse and that our generation will not live to see the end of it nor even the worst of it, Mark speaks: "Look at the beginning. It was mess then. Read your own story, the history of Christ's church. Has it ever been other? Yet it is the divine mess, the dough God is mixing. In our weakness, there is strength; in our failure there is hope. For in the midst of our mess there is God, and through our enduring comes the Love that endures. The Christians in Rome knew that the message of the empty tomb, which had caused the women to flee at first in fear, had nonetheless reached Rome and was spreading all over the empire. We for our part can reflect that Rome is still the eternal city and that the gospel is what has made Rome the eternal city. As we approach 2000 C.E., if we know history at all well, we know that the history of the church these two thousand years has been the history of failure and mess. But the gospel does endure. If we feel now that the church is going down, that feeling too has surfaced many times these past two millennia. If the reign of God as we would like it to look is heart-rendingly absent, that does not mean that God's reign has perished from the earth. It simply means that God's reign is coming in ways we are not used to.

The quotation above comes from the first part of Chesterton's ballad. It is entitled "The Vision of the King." Alfred of Wessex— that oft-defeated king, he calls himself—has been granted a vision of Our Lady. Alfred is setting out to muster the Anglo-Saxon tribes to fight once more against the Viking invader. Alfred tells Our Lady that he will not seek from her heaven's secrets, but there is one small thing he would know from her. When this battle is over, will Wessex be free at last from the pagan warriors. The answer Our Lady gives captures beautifully Mark's message to us who, at the end of the second millennium bear the Good News.

The gates of heaven are lightly locked,
we do not guard our gold,
men may uproot where worlds begin,
or read the name of the nameless sin;
but if he fail or if he win
to no good man is told.

The men of the East may spell the stars,
and times and triumphs mark,
but the men signed of the cross of Christ
go gaily in the dark.

The men of the East may search the scrolls
for sure fates and fame.
But the men that drink the blood of God
go singing to their shame.

The wise men know what wicked things
are written in the sky,
They trim sad lamps, they touch sad strings,
hearing the heavy purple wings
where the forgotten seraph kings
still plot how God shall die.
The wise men know all evil things
under the twisted trees,
where the perverse in pleasure pine
and men are weary of green wine
and sick of crimson seas.

But you and all the kind of Christ
are ignorant and brave,
and you have wars you hardly win
and souls you hardly save.

I tell you naught for your comfort
yea, naught for your desire,
save that the sky grows darker yet
and the sea rises higher.

Night shall be thrice night over you,
and heaven an iron cope.
Do you have joy without a cause,
yea, faith without a hope?

As we enter the third millennium we need to do so humbly, realizing that very much remains that is still to be accomplished. The Good News about Jesus, the Christ, the Son of God, is hardly yet begun.

NOTES

1. For the most part those who argue that Matthew was written first also argue that Matthew wrote that Gospel in the early to mid-forties. The *need* to have a written Gospel very much closer to the time of Jesus' ministry (Jesus died probably in 30 C.E.) indicates fundamentalist leanings.

2. For example, there seems to be no purpose served in Matthew's second feeding episode. He has avoided Mark's meaning—bread for the Gentiles—yet feels compelled to include the episode so as to be faithful to Mark.

3. Augustine thought that the Fourth Gospel presumed that the reader already had the story from another Gospel, though he does not specify which one. I should note here that Raymond Brown, one of the greatest Catholic biblical scholars, and certainly one who can speak with very great authority about the Fourth Gospel, does not feel any need to suppose that the author of the Fourth Gospel was familiar with any of the earlier Gospels.

4. See John Meier and Raymond Brown, *Antioch and Rome* (New York: Paulist Press, 1983), 111.

5. Ibid., 139–58.

6. The *Shepherd of Hermas,* a later document from Rome, also quotes from Mark. See S. E. Johnson, *Commentary on the Gospel of Mark* (London: Black-Harper, 1960), 7.

7. Adolf Hitler is recorded as having said that "taken to its logical extreme, Christianity would mean the systematic cultivation of human failure" (see Alan Bullock, *Hitler and Stalin: Parallel Lives* [London: Fontana Press, 1993], 412). Possibly he had an insight into Christianity that the triumphalist church lacked. Nevertheless, he did not understand. Jesus' failure is because God embraced us in our mess. If the human story

had been different, the story of Jesus (and the story of the church) would also have been different. Hitler admired the Catholic Church, not for the gospel but for the power of its organization. I believe that the fundamental struggle within the church now is between those who want a return to that strong church, and those who want to follow the gospel faithfully, leaving questions of strength or weakness, success or failure in God's hands. But simply to divide Catholics up into one category or the other would be as dangerous as it is to divide the human race simply into Catholics and non-Catholics, Jew and Goy, insiders and outsiders.

8. See *The Collected Poems of G. K. Chesterton,* 12th ed. (London: Methuen & Co., 1950), 233.

BIBLIOGRAPHY

WORKS CITED

Aland, Kurt, Matthew Black, Carlo M. Martini, Bruce M. Metzger, and Allen Wikgren, eds. *Nestle-Aland 26th Edition: The Greek New Testament.* 3rd ed. (corrected). New York: United Bible Societies, 1966, 1968, 1975, 1982.

Bailey, Kenneth E. *Through Peasant Eyes.* Grand Rapids, Mich.: William B. Eerdmans, 1980.

Béguerie, Philippe, and Claude Duchesneau. *How to Understand the Sacraments.* London: SCM Press, 1991.

Brown, Raymond E., S.S. *The Death of the Messiah.* Anchor Bible Reference Library. New York: Doubleday, 1994.

———. *An Introduction to New Testament Christology.* New York/Mahwah, N.J.: Paulist Press, 1994.

Corsini, Eugenio, S.D.B. *The Apocalypse: The Perennial Revelation of Jesus Christ.* Translated by Francis Moloney, S.D.B. Good News Studies 5. Wilmington, Del.: Michael Glazier, 1983.

Daly, Robert J., S.J. *The Origins of Christian Sacrifice.* Philadelphia: Fortress Press, 1978.

Dewey, Joanna. *Markan Public Debate: Literary Technique, Concentric Structure, and Theology of Mark 2:1-3:6.* Society of Biblical Literature Dissertation Series 48. Chico, Calif.: Scholars Press, 1980.

Johnson, S. E. *Commentary on the Gospel of Mark.* London: Black-Harper, 1960.

Lohmeyer, E. *Das Evangelium nach Markus.* Göttingen: Vandenhoeck & Ruprecht, 1937.

Martin, Ralph. *Mark, Evangelist and Theologian.* Grand Rapids, Mich.: Zondervan, 1973.

187

Meier, John, and Raymond Brown. *Antioch and Rome*. New York: Paulist Press, 1983.

Myers, Ched. *Binding the Strong Man: A Political Reading of Mark's Story of Jesus*. Maryknoll, N.Y.: Orbis Books, 1988.

Stevenson, J. *A New Eusebius: Documents Illustrating the History of the Church to AD 337*. New edition revised by W. H. C. Frend. London: SPCK, 1987.

Stock, Augustine. *Call to Discipleship*. Good News Studies 1. Wilmington, Del.: Michael Glazier, 1982.

Taylor, Vincent. *The Gospel According to Mark*. Thornapple Commentaries. 2nd ed. Grand Rapids, Mich.: Baker Book House, 1981.

Zerwick, Max, and Mary Grosvenor. *A Grammatical Analysis of the New Testament*. Rome: Biblical Institute Press, 1981.

RECOMMENDED FOR BEGINNERS FOR FURTHER STUDY

Burdon, Christopher. *Stumbling on God*. London: SPCK, 1990.

Matera, Frank J. *What Are They Saying about Mark?* New York/Mahwah, N.J.: Paulist Press, 1987.

Montague, George T. *Mark: Good News for Hard Times*. Ann Arbor, Mich.: Servant Books, 1981.

Senior, Donald. *The Gospel of Saint Mark*. NCR Cassettes for Religious Education Courses. Kansas City, Mo.: National Catholic Reporter, 1977.

———. *The Passion of Jesus in the Gospel of Mark*. Wilmington, Del.: Michael Glazier, 1984.

Stock, Augustine. *Call to Discipleship*. Good News Studies 1. Wilmington, Del.: Michael Glazier, 1982.